TIMOTHY H. JOYCE

SWIMMING HOLES

OF CALIFORNIA

For information, contact Sierra Publications.

First Printing, June 2013

ISBN-13: 978-1490456874

ISBN-10: 1490456872

Acknowledgments

Thanks to my friends and family for their support and encouragement. A special thanks goes to Tom Hillegass for his contributions regarding safety. For further information about Tom or his website, please visit:

http://www.swimmingholes.org

Sierra Publications Staff

Author & Photographer: Timothy H. Joyce

Design & Layout: Edwar Martinez & Thomas White

Book cover diver: Michael Goodrich. Photo and permission by Jeffrey Goodrich.

Cover: Clockwise from bottom left, Oregon Creek, God's Bath, Webber Creek (private).

Table Of Contents

SHASTA & TRINITY

HUMBOLDT, MENDOCINO & THE REDWOODS

CHICO, PLUMAS & THE FEATHER RIVER

GOLD COUNTRY & YUBA RIVER

SANTA CRUZ & BOLINAS

THE SEQUOIAS

BIG SUR, SALINAS & SANTA BARBARA

Author's Note

Hiking is a potentially dangerous activity. Some areas in this book may require special care and attention or require traversing unmaintained areas or trails that can present risks. When possible always hike with another person. Further, do not venture off into the wilderness alone or without leaving proper notification with a friend or relative. Certain hikes and approaches in this book may require a person to be in good physical shape to avoid risk or injury. Further, although this book tries to point out dangers and risks, conditions can and do change on a yearly, seasonal, and even weekly basis. Seasonal indicators are provided as a guideline and are by no way a guarantee of safety for swimming. Always bring sufficient water and food to avoid starvation and dehydration. Many people drown or are injured by jumping from rocks and cliffs. This should be avoided. Never enter a swimming hole without making a careful and thoughtful analysis of the river, and areas above and below the water line. Rocks in the river can be steep and slippery. Proper hiking and water attire are a must. However, such equipment by no way will guarantee safety from slipping, falling, or being injured.

The swimming holes provided in this book are largely on public land. A few may cross or lie close to private property. In all cases you should obey (no trespassing) signs and landowner property rights.

In summary, you are on your own out there, and you assume all the associated risks. Use your head and plan ahead. Stay safe and most of all, have fun!

Courtesy of Gilbert Lemke
Left to right: Adrian Lemke, Andrew Levitt, Julia Lemke
South Fork of Yuba River, near Washington, CA

Swimming Hole Safety!

Swimming holes and hiking to them can be great fun. However, they do present some safety issues that you should be aware of. Swimming holes are unique in that they can display different personalities depending upon the time you visit them.

For instance, God's Bath on the Clavey River at the end of August can be calm and easy to reach. Try doing the same hike in April and you might regret it.

For this reason, make sure that you properly research the places you plan on hiking to. Books like this and others can provide valuable resources to begin your planning. Further, when you get to the swimming hole, do not jump right in! First you should test the water to see how fast it's moving. This can be easily done by dropping a leaf or stick into the water and seeing how fast it floats away. If it floats more than 10 yards away before you can put your water shoes on, then it's too fast. Stay away from fast moving waters. They will only get you into trouble.

Most drownings in swimming holes are due to strong currents, diving, and/or alcohol. Do not let carelessness or peer pressure get you into a situation you cannot handle. Each time you go, wade in gradually and check the current. Do not jump in until you have checked both the depth and the current first. NEVER dive in head first. Do not go in if you see any tree branches or other debris in the water.

Large rivers have hidden currents below the surface — assume large rivers are NEVER safe to swim regardless of how calm they look on the surface.

If you find yourself being swept away in a current, DO NOT PANIC AND DO NOT FIGHT THE CURRENT — float feet first downstream on your back. Let the current carry you until it becomes gentle and/or until you calm down. While floating on your back and still facing feet first downstream, gradually use your arms to swim to shore. If you swim or boat in creeks often, you should practice this maneuver until it becomes familiar.

PLEASE, NEVER, EVER:

- Dive head first (paralysis, death);

- Swim alone;

- Drink alcohol and swim;

- Go barefoot (glass, sharp rocks);

- Stand directly under a waterfall (rocks wash over falls);

- Swim in upper pools of a waterfall (you wash over falls);

- Climb above or alongside a waterfall (many deaths from this);

- Try to stand up in strong currents (feet get trapped in bottom rocks and current holds you down.)

- Instead, float on your back with feet downstream until the current subsides.

FOLLOW THESE ADDED PRECAUTIONS:

- Don't put your hands or feet into places you can't see (snake dangers).

- Be careful when on a rope swing.

Wild Animals & Snakes!

Mountain lions, bears, and other wild animals can from time to time present safety concerns. Just like a bad in-law, when you least expect them, they will show up! For this reason, you should plan ahead. For instance, having a walking stick or knife for protection is a good start. If you know you are going into bear territory, you should carry bear mace for protection.

Probably the fastest way to clear out any swimming hole, is to yell the word "snake." The author was swimming in a crowded swimming hole one summer when he thought he saw a snake in the water. He then yelled "snake." Luckily it was confirmed to be a floating stick. By the time the author looked up, though, the entire swimming hole was cleared out. Never mention the "S" word unless you have to.

Most interesting about this incident was that most people are ignorant regarding how to deal with snakes and treat snakebites. For instance, one teenager swimming by assured the other swimmers that rattlesnakes can't swim. No reason to be alarmed, since it must be a nonpoisonous water snake. DEAD WRONG! Rattlesnakes are good swimmers. One just needs to search on Google for the numerous examples. Rattlesnakes are generally shy and will avoid humans. About 98% of snakebites comprise owners of snakes and young teenage boys that have already spotted the snake, but decided they wanted to play a game. The best way to deal with snakes is to avoid them. If you see a snake, assume it's poisonous and stay away! It's just too hard for most people to determine whether it's a water snake, gopher snake, or rattlesnake. On the rare occasion that you do encounter or get bit by a snake, here is an excerpt from an article by John Henkel titled "Treating and Preventing Venomous Snakebites."

Avoiding Snakebites

Some bites, such as those inflicted when snakes are accidentally stepped on or encountered in wilderness settings, are nearly impossible to prevent. But experts say a few precautions can lower the risk of being bitten:

- Leave snakes alone. Many people are bitten because they try to kill a snake or get a closer look at it.

- Stay out of tall grass unless you wear thick leather boots, and remain on hiking paths as much as possible.

- Keep hands and feet out of areas you can't see. Don't pick up rocks or firewood unless you are out of a snake's striking distance. (A snake can strike half its length, Hardy says.)

- Be cautious and alert when climbing rocks.

What do you do if you encounter a snake when hiking or picnicking? Says Hardy: "Just walk around the snake, giving it a little berth — six feet is plenty. But leave it alone and don't try to catch it."

First Aid for Snakebites

Over the years, snakebite victims have been exposed to all kinds of slicing, freezing, and squeezing as stopgap measures before receiving medical care. Some of these approaches like cutting into a bite and attempting to suck out the venom, have largely fallen out of favor. "In the past five or 10 years, there's been a backing off in first aid from really invasive things like making incisions," says Arizona physician David Hardy, M.D., who studies snakebite epidemiology. "This is because we now know these things can do harm and we don't know if they really change the outcome." Many health-care professionals embrace just a few basic first- aid techniques. According to the American Red Cross, these steps should be taken.

- Wash the bite with soap and water.

- Immobilize the bitten area and keep it lower than the heart.

- Get medical help.

"The main thing is to get to a hospital and don't delay," says Hardy. "Most bites don't occur in real isolated situations, so it's feasible to get prompt medical care." He describes cases in Arizona where people have caught rattlesnakes for sport and gotten bitten. "They waited until they couldn't stand the pain anymore and finally went to the hospital after the venom had been in there a few hours. But by then, they'd lost an opportunity for effective treatment," which increased the odds of long-term complications. Some medical professionals, along with the American Red Cross, cautiously recommend two other measures:

- If a victim is unable to reach medical care within 30 minutes, a bandage, wrapped two to four inches above the bite, may help slow venom. The bandage should not cut off blood flow from a vein or artery. A good rule of thumb is to make the band loose enough that a finger can slip under it.

- Do not panic, walk slowly and keep the snakebite area below the heart.

- Mark the time next to the location of the bite.

- If the snake is dead then bag it for later identification.

- If the snake is not dead, leave it alone, but note the color, shape, and markings.

- Suction devices are largely considered not effective. If effective at all, they must be used within the first five minutes of the snakebite.

Many snakebites are "dry bites." That means they do not inject any venom. You will know within 15 minutes if it's a "wet" or "dry" bite based on the inflammation and swelling. Contrary to what most people believe, the baby rattlesnakes present a bigger risk than some larger rattlesnakes, because they don't know how to control the levels of their venom.

How NOT to Treat a Snakebite

Though U.S. medical professionals may not agree on every aspect of what to do for snakebite first aid, they are nearly unanimous in their views of what not to do. Among their recommendations:

- No ice or any other type of cooling on the bite. Research has shown this to be potentially harmful.

- No tourniquets. This cuts blood flow completely and may result in loss of the affected limb.

- No electric shock. This method is under study and has yet to be proven effective. It could harm the victim.

- No incisions in the wound. Such measures have not been proven useful and may cause further injury.

Arizona physician David Hardy, M.D., says part of the problem when someone is bitten is the element of surprise. "People often aren't trained in what to do, and they are in a panic situation." He adds that preparation that includes knowing in advance how to get to the nearest hospital could greatly reduce anxiety and lead to more effective care.

ROPE SWING CAUTION!

There are more accidents from rope swings than the average person could imagine. Always test the rope first before using it. This can be done by pulling on the rope and placing your entire body weight on it to see if it can hold. This is no guarantee, so always assume the rope might break. A few additional precautions regarding rope swings include:

- Always enter the water feet first.

- Wet hands and wet ropes can be a slippery combination — make sure you have a good grip on the rope.

- Be sure it's deep enough below and there are no hidden rocks.

- If there are any loops in the rope, NEVER put your hand or foot or any other part of your body in the loop — just hold on with your hands.

- Especially for children — make sure they know that they HAVE TO LET GO and cannot swing back on the rope where they will very likely hit something.

Oregon Creek, Yuba County, CA

Everything's working out perfectly. The guys are at the swimming hole, and I'm home with a toothache. Nothing could possibly go wrong.

-Little Rascals

Forward

This book is different from other swimming hole and waterfall books. It's designed to easily locate important information for any hiker or swimming hole enthusiast that is on the run. However, it also provides added details if one desires to gather more information before visiting a particular place. Most important to a swimming hole enthusiast are clear and accurate directions and big and beautiful color pictures. Pictures make a swimming hole book. They provide the "vision" of the slice of paradise one wants to visit and enjoy. The first thing almost anyone does when they buy a swimming holes book is to begin to thumb through the pages to look at the pictures and determine what is the best swimming hole and where is it located. We have already done this work for you. This entire book features the best of the best swimming holes in California.

What makes a great swimming hole? Although that can be quite personal for some, we believe most people prefer rock slides and/or tubs carved out of granite, beautiful flowing falls, a strong vertical (jumps or cliffs for jumping) or horizontal component (sandy beach with Alders), hikes long enough to get away from civilization, but not so far as to tire one out, clean clear water, limited crowds, and no man made obstructions. Further, we think many people want to be able to get to the swimming hole with limited hassle.

As mentioned, an important component to a great swimming hole is that it can't be so close to civilization that it feels more like the city pool. In contrast, swimming holes that we found to be greater than 4-mile hikes one way (greater than 8-mile hikes) just weren't worth all the extra effort. We often found hikes to be rushed to get to the hole and then a few minutes dip and a quick hike back to get home before dark. That just was not that fun either. For these reasons, we only feature the best of the best swimming holes that can be reached on a day trip and are no further than 8 miles round trip.

Nothing is more daunting than a bad "approach." When we say approach we mean the road to the swimming hole. Most people want to know what they are up against and don't want to get stuck on a lousy road driving miles on edge hoping they won't breakdown, bottom out, or get stuck. For this reason, we provide detailed information regarding the roads and what to expect so enthusiasts can plan accordingly. We also have conducted extensive research to determine the best roads and simplest routes to get to a destination. In most cases, we have provided directions on slightly longer routes that were paved and more pleasant drives, than risk directing travel over shorter unpaved and bumpy roads.

Last, and most important, swimming holes change. They are not static, but dynamic. Changes can be physical or in approach. For instance, some swimming holes can become shallow due to sand deposits by winter rain storms. In other cases, some landowners may block easements or access to once public swimming holes. For this reason, we maintain an active and informative website that is free of charge. We continually visit swimming holes, and interact with our enthusiasts. Feel free to contact us through the site if you have any questions or need information about any swimming holes we may not have featured. We are at:

http://swimmingholesofcalifornia.blogspot.com.

Also, check out some of our HD videos. They are posted on our website. We hope you enjoy the book and the swimming holes.

Best of luck!

Timothy H. Joyce

Introduction

It all began years ago attending a small camp in Lovell, Maine. Hiking in the White Mountains was always great fun. However, the best hikes always had a swimming hole. The most glorious of them all was "Emerald Pool" near Caribou Mountain in New Hampshire. None of us could remember how to get there or even where it was, but it was our secret swimming hole. That was important. That is what made it so legendary. The beautiful high rock walls, the solitude, and most of all the "cold" clean emerald-colored water. The type of water so cold you could jump in for just a minute or two and come out all "red." The water was so clear you could drop a quarter to the bottom and still be able to read the mint mark on it.

Almost everyone has a swimming hole they try to keep secret. It just seems to go with the territory. Stock brokers have their stocks, attorneys their privileges, and hikers their swimming holes. On more than one occasion the author personally experienced wrong or bad directions to a swimming hole. This leads one to wonder if the directions were by mistake or intentional to maintain the secrecy of the swimming hole. On other occasions the author has viewed what one would call the "local" vs. "flatlander" approach where the locals prefer not to share their knowledge for fear that their sacred swimming hole could be "trashed" or would become overrun with thugs or outsiders that do not respect and take care of their space. However, one of the greatest sources of fun and excitement is sharing the swimming hole experience.

When the author moved to California, it just seemed natural to get out and hike. Everyone seems to do it. It's just part of the entire experience and a way of life. Hiking though can get hot and tiring. So what better way to enjoy the experience than by hiking to a swimming hole. Hiking to swimming holes can become addictive. Once you have enjoyed a few, you catch the "bug" and are hooked for good. There just isn't anything so rewarding as getting out and exercising in the great outdoors.

Oddly enough though, it's not the hike distance, or surroundings that make swimming holes so appealing. It's the rock formations, the tubs, the slides, and the waterfalls. They add a special element that is just too good to resist.

The hard rock and granite in California, combined with the seasonal rainfalls provide ideal conditions for building and maintaining swimming holes. Further, swimming holes can get stagnant or filled with debris. Each year, mother nature then cleans them for each new swim season.

If you have ever hiked to one or more swimming holes, you quickly learn the golden rule regarding swimming holes. It's hard to find swimming holes. The author can't tell you how many times he has had a map, GPS, and compass, and it has taken hours to locate a single swimming hole. Sometimes the author had to go back two to three times to try to locate the same swimming hole.

In the end, swimming holes are for everyone who wants to enjoy and respect them. They are for kids, for families, and for couples wishing to find their own romantic getaway.

Last, nothing is worse than setting off on a weekend drive to reach a hike or swimming hole destination, to realize that you can't locate it, or worse get lost. For this reason, in this book we provide detailed Google maps, GPS coordinates, and highly detailed directions.

We hope you will enjoy the swimming holes in California as much as we do. Happy hunting!

Using The Book

Many hiking and guide books take a small area and give lots of details regarding the trails or topography. In this text we provide a more general approach using Google maps and instructions. In some situations, Google Earth is so detailed that it was possible to locate the swimming hole without even scouting first. We believe this is the best information to help in locating swimming holes. The book is also laid out in a simple and easy approach to follow. We have also supplemented the material with important information such as the existence of nearby restrooms, restaurants, etc. We believe this information is necessary to round out a book on swimming holes.

Given that it's often difficult to locate some swimming holes, we have included Google maps with relative GPS coordinates. We have found the GPS coordinates to be helpful in locating most swimming holes in California. Most swimming holes we have been able to successfully locate coordinates and signal using even the simplest devices. We also make recommendations regarding some equipment one might want consider as one becomes a swimming hole enthusiast.

The swimming holes in this book are rated according to a numerical rating system. The ratings are from 1 to 10. For instance, a rating of 1 is the lowest and a rating of 10 being the highest. Although we provide the best of the best swimming holes in California, we appreciate that some enthusiasts have limited time and, therefore, want to cut to the chase in getting to the best swimming holes.

None of the swimming holes in this book require rock climbing skills. We have tried to limit the hikes and approaches to those places that are enjoyable and somewhat safe. Although in many cases climbing on or around rocks may be required. Further, in some cases some approaches may be steep. However, all of them have trails that have been worn or used. Further, none require the use of ropes. Some may be difficult for older people or young children. In other cases, some of the swimming holes may have steep granite slabs that can present a danger. However, there are generally other approaches that provide a safer alternative.

The Hike & Trails

These designations tell how long or difficult the approach or hike is.

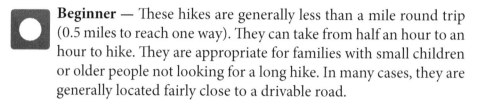 **Beginner** — These hikes are generally less than a mile round trip (0.5 miles to reach one way). They can take from half an hour to an hour to hike. They are appropriate for families with small children or older people not looking for a long hike. In many cases, they are generally located fairly close to a drivable road.

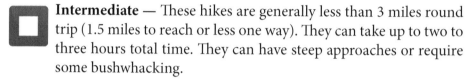 **Intermediate** — These hikes are generally less than 3 miles round trip (1.5 miles to reach or less one way). They can take up to two to three hours total time. They can have steep approaches or require some bushwhacking.

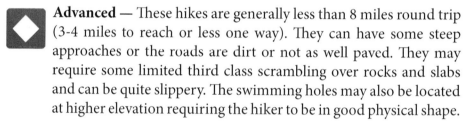 **Advanced** — These hikes are generally less than 8 miles round trip (3-4 miles to reach or less one way). They can have some steep approaches or the roads are dirt or not as well paved. They may require some limited third class scrambling over rocks and slabs and can be quite slippery. The swimming holes may also be located at higher elevation requiring the hiker to be in good physical shape.

We do not include swimming holes in this book beyond an 8-mile range. We have found that these hikes are generally beyond the level of most swimming hole enthusiasts and require more extensive planning to reach and return in one day. Most people when confronted with such a hike will opt to go to another and more easily approachable swimming hole. We also have eliminated those swimming holes that would present a serious danger to a hiker or enthusiast. Most of the swimming hole trailheads in this text can be reached with a regular automobile.

The Season & Time

We use actual months within the top information areas. Each swimming hole can be different and for this reason we have provided months for clear distinctions that may not be evident from an icon alone. Further, icons alone require referencing back and forth within a text. We have made it easier for the reader by providing this information on the same page.

If you want to enjoy the beauty of a spot or are into photography, visiting swimming holes can be a year-round adventure. However, if you enjoy the swimming it's helpful to know the best seasons. We have found that some swimming holes by their very nature are going to be cold. For instance, many of the best swimming holes result from snow or glacier run off. This places them in a special category. We call them so cold that even a polar bear would complain. As a whole, therefore, season becomes a highly relevant issue. Cold water can be highly refreshing if the hike to the swimming hole is somewhat hot or moderately arduous.

Beyond that we believe there is a point of diminishing returns. For these reasons, we provide both subjective information regarding water temperature and season.

In California, the swimming hole season generally begins in June and ends at the end of September. Earlier than June the water is too cold for many people and the water levels due to runoff can be quite rapid and dangerous. After September, the runoff and flow levels can be quite slow. Some pools become stagnant or collect debris.

As a note on safety, never swim in water that is rapidly moving or at high flows. In addition, you should stay well back from the edge of the river. In California, this would be in the months of January to April. These months tend to be the high runoff times where many people slip into the river and drown. The Kern River is particularly notorious for the lives it has claimed. There is a sign at the road that enters the canyon listing the number of drowning deaths. At the time of publication of this book it's around 240 lives.

It should also be noted that in Southern California the season is slightly different and shorter. The water temperature is also slightly warmer. Although, not by much. Southern California is really a spring thing. In other words, their swimming season begins in March and ends at the beginning of June since runoff levels diminish quite quickly.

We use seasonal designations as follows:

 Spring — Smaller or dryer watersheds. These swimming holes open in March or April and generally close at the end of June. Most of the swimming holes in Southern California follow this classification.

 Summer — This is the season where most of the swimming holes in California can be enjoyed. The season is typically from the Fourth of July until Labor Day or end of August. Beyond August either the water becomes stagnant in some cases, or the weather becomes too cold at higher elevation.

 Fall — This is generally the month of September and possibly into the first week of October. Only a few rare cases meet this classification. We provide this for the enthusiast who wishes to extend the swimming season just a little bit longer than usual.

It should be noted that some swimming holes may have dual or multiple designations. They can be enjoyed during various months and we have listed those months in the informational areas.

People & Preferences

This group of icons shows the company you will encounter at some of these swimming holes. It also identifies some of their preferences and whether to expect crowds or privacy.

 Kids — This icon indicates whether the swimming hole is appropriate for kids under the age of 7 years old. These swimming holes are generally fairly easy to reach and have somewhat easier approaches.

 Dogs & Pets — This icon indicates whether the trails and swimming holes are pet friendly. In California, some of the parks are dog or pet friendly. In many cases, they are not. They are not pet friendly in two regards. First of all, the Forest Service may not allow it. The second reason is that some trails are steep in areas that require climbing and four legs just can't seem to make it at certain points. We, therefore, particularly identify those locations that allow animals and meet both considerations.

 Boom Box, Bikini, & Beer Brat Battalions — Crowds are likely. These swimming holes can be crowded and noisy. The have more of a feel of a city beach. There may be young girls in bikinis strutting their stuff or boys showing off their muscles and tattoos. Families may be present having picnics or barbeques. There may be the drinking of alcoholic beverages.

 Public nudity — Although many swimming holes can motivate one to want to shuck off one's clothes, this icon indicates those places where nudity tends to be a norm. It may not be appropriate for junior. For instance, at the side beach of the Garden of Eden in Santa Cruz, on more than one occasion the author has been confronted with entire families in the raw. These nudity areas may or may not be legally zoned this way. The text points out those areas that are legally zoned for such activities. It also points out those places where visual surprises are possible.

The Facilities & Equipment

No swimming hole book would be complete without information regarding facilities and equipment. Just like any good guide you might hire to get you where you are going, it's also nice to be provided with information regarding the presence or absence of bathrooms, gas stations, and restaurants. Further, some hikes can be fairly rigorous and hot and require water. The author has found the average hiker typically just decides to "go" with little thought or planning about water, food, and protection. On more than one occasion the author has found members of his own group forgetting to bring enough water, or even bring some water at all. After all, we are hiking to a swimming hole and there is plenty of water! Nothing could be further from the truth.

Many swimming holes are at high elevation or in steep hot canyons requiring special planning with food and water. It's no fun misjudging a hike and wondering if you are going to make it back to your car before dehydration has set in. For these reasons, we provide information regarding important planning considerations and point out places where the canyons can get really hot.

 Bathrooms — This icon indicates the presence of bathrooms nearby or near the trailhead. In the case where bathrooms are not at the trailhead they are within 2 miles of the trailhead.

 Gas up — The red icon indicates a need to get gasoline and gas up prior to going to the swimming hole. In certain cases, this means that the closest services could be 10 miles or more away. If you run out of gas or do not plan properly you could be walking a long distance.

 Gas Station — The green icon indicates the presence of a gas station nearby or at a local town near the swimming hole.

 Restaurants — This icon indicates the existence of food and restaurants within 10 miles of the trailhead. Where appropriate some recommendations may be provided. In certain instances the icon may also indicate the presence or existence of a supermarket within the prescribed boundaries.

Biking — Some swimming holes may be reached by bike. In some cases a bike might be more effective in traveling on a dirt road. We point out those places that offer the ability to cost effectively rent a bike or allow for the use of bikes on the trail.

 Water — This icon indicates the need to plan and bring extra water. The associated hike and/or canyon can be quite hot or is at high elevation which can quickly lead to exhaustion and dehydration.

 Cactus — This icon indicates the presence of hot climate conditions, an area that needs to be crossed that is like a desert, or canyons that can reach extreme heat. This icon provides a warning to plan ahead with proper attire, sun screen, and water.

 Climbing — This icon indicates a steep approach or portion of the hike that can be somewhat challenging. None of the approaches to the swimming holes described here require ropes. However, some may require some climbing or bouldering.

 Snake — This icon indicates the need to take proper precautions for snakes. The hike or approach may cross fields, gullies, or wooded areas where boots would be a good option.

 Camping — This icon indicates camping is possible near the swimming hole or in the close vicinity.

Hiking to swimming holes does not require any particular equipment. However, there is certain equipment that will make your trips more enjoyable and possibly safer. Most of the equipment we recommend can be purchased from many online sites. Other places like your local back packing or outdoors store like REI® should carry the equipment we recommend.

Hiking Boots & Socks — If you haven't yet invested in a pair of hiking boots, you might want to consider this soon. A good pair of hiking boots and socks are worth their weight in gold. They will prevent knee, foot, and ankle injuries and will make the hikes more enjoyable. We recommend low cut hiking boots with a sturdy sole. They should be durable, breathable, and capable of easy removal. For instance, some trails may require the hiker to cross water or stand on wet rocks. A sturdy and non-slip rubber on the sole of the boot will help prevent falls and slips. For instance, Vasque® makes a sole with very good traction on even wet terrain. In addition, on occasion it may be necessary to remove the shoes to cross a river or slab, so they must be light enough to carry. Thick, breathable, and comfortable socks are also a necessity when walking distances greater than 2 miles. Brands similar to SmartWool® might be good bets.

Water Shoes — There are many different types of water shoes. They come in all kinds of shapes, textures, colors, and sizes. The best ones will allow water to access and drain easily. In addition, they should prevent sand and other debris from collecting in the bottom of the shoe and toe. The shoes must be capable of tightening and removal and should be lightweight so you can swim with them on. Water shoes will be invaluable and necessary if you plan to jump from rocks or cliffs into the water. They cushion the fall and prevent injuries if by chance you are to touch bottom. Most important about water shoes is the quality of the rubber used. If you frequent swimming holes you will quickly learn that most of the rocks and slabs can be quite slippery and dangerous. Climbing in bare feet or with regular water shoes will not work very well. A number of manufacturers make water shoes with "high stick" or soft rubbers. For instance, Teva® makes a water shoe that comprises "Spider Rubber®." The first time the author tried these shoes he was amazed. When they are wet they are designed to stick even better. These shoes make climbing on rocks, slabs, and steep ravines a real joy. We strongly recommend that you look into a similar type of shoe to avoid slips and falls. Teva® "Spider Rubber®" shoes can be purchased at an outdoor store such as REI®.

Swim Suits & Shorts — Hiking to a swimming hole can provide a certain dilemma. Do I wear a bathing suit or shorts? Wear the bathing suit under the shorts? The answer to the question is neither. The technology is to the point that "wicking shorts" are the new wave. These are shorts or swimwear made of non-absorbing nanomaterial or polyester. They dry almost within minutes. This makes hiking and long drives much more enjoyable since you don't have to sit for hours in damp shorts or have to change in the car by doing the "bathing suit wiggle." We strongly recommend that you invest in a pair or two of these shorts. Many of the shorts and shirts also provide UV protection. We recommend a light color. Anything but black should work fine. Black will absorb sunlight and make you hot really fast.

Towels — On more than one occasion the author has personally observed some of the world's largest towels being packed for swimming hole hikes. These towels provide little advantage and often soak up lots of water making them a ton to carry. The new technology now provides "wicking" towels that will dry within minutes. Some of these towels come with a carry case and can easily fit into a pocket. How about that!

Sun Gear & Protection — Often overlooked, but almost more important than the bathing suit. A hat is almost always a good choice to help reduce sun exposure. Sunglasses are also very important. In California, the sun exposure and glare can be quite high. Unless you want to spend most of your time squinting, we recommend that you invest in a good pair of shades. We also recommend that you don't go on the cheap with the shades. Eye protection needs to protect your eyes yet not be so expensive that their loss or damage would cause mental anguish. You also want to invest in a pair of sunglasses that are useful for outdoor activities. We are not talking about the Versace® or other high-end sunglasses that look good. We are talking more about purchasing a pair of Oakley's® or similar quality. Oakley® is on the cutting edge with their sunglasses. Almost all sunglasses are required to block UVA and B sunlight. Oakley® is the only manufacturer that certifies their sunglasses can block the deeply penetrating and damaging UVC rays. Oakley® sunglasses can be a little pricey, but hey, it's your eyes. Oakley® also is one of those manufacturers that stand behind their sunglasses. You can't go wrong there.

There are many types of sunblock on the market. The author has researched many of the companies and products. Recent research indicates that sunblock is only effective up to 30 SPF. In other words, products claiming to have higher level protection are not telling the complete story. In addition, nothing is more annoying than sweating and have sunblock get in your eyes causing the blurring sting. If you can't understand or speak the words on the sunblock, you might want to try something else. Research indicates the most effective ingredient in sunblock is zinc oxide. Yeah, that is the white stuff you sometimes see on surfer or volleyball players at the beach. Look for a sunblock with at least 18-20% zinc or titanium oxide present (can be in combination). Not really much more is needed as ingredients. You will get the best sun protection and will avoid that nasty blurring burn. We recommend an Eco-sensitive, biodegradable, PABA, Paraben, and petroleum-free sunblock such as Burn Out® or Dr. Perry's Natural Block®. Dr. Perry's® can be ordered over the internet. Burn Out® is manufactured by a company in Santa Cruz, California, and can be purchased at a store such as Whole Foods®.

Cameras — Various pocket size and SLR cameras are available. Many can last for hours and provide great photos. Unless you really enjoy photography, a pocket camera should be just fine. However, if you are considering video-taping your trips, you might consider investing in a camera such as a lighter weight SLR that can provide both great photos and HD video capabilities.

GPS Navigation System — On more than one occasion we've been asked what GPS system to purchase. We personally consider the special hiking units a waste of money. We've looked at them and they just aren't there yet with the technology. The standard over-the-counter GPS units work just fine. There are various manufacturers and they all seem to work fairly well. We particularly like the Garmin units because of the software and their ease to pack and carry. We also recommend a service plan.

Camelbak® — If you haven't bought a Camelbak® for hiking you should do so now. There is no better way to carry food, supplies, and water. We recommend the largest two- to three-liter size. You can then scale things back if you need to. It really beats carrying those bottles in your hands.

Bug Balms & Repellents — Most of the swimming holes in California do not have issues with bugs. However, certain times of the year and places can experience such problems. We, therefore, provide some suggestions for those sensitive types that seem to attract all the black flies. We strongly recommend against anything that has DEET. That is a nasty word that does damage to your skin and the environment. Instead, choose more appealing brands like Badger Balm® that use effective natural components like Citronella.

Aches & Pains — Regardless of the shape you are in, we all experience sore muscles, joint pains, and tightness. The author strongly recommends that you go to your local health food store such as Whole Foods® and purchase a bottle of tart cherry juice concentrate and/or coconut water. Note: sweet cherry juice will not work. It must be tart! Tart cherry juice is a miracle remedy. It has been used to treat gout and other arthritis conditions. You simply mix a small amount with some water and drink it. You will not have any pains or aches before or after your hike! Further, if you are really health conscious, you can mix it with some coconut water, which is high in potassium.

Miscellaneous — Here is a list of various optional items you can store in your car: first aid kit, a 12-pack or more of bottled water, extra tooth brushes, rain gear, some baggies for storing wet or dirty shoes, some hand wipes for wipe downs after the hike, a knife, Mace or bear protectant, a pair of snake boots, umbrella, towels, and some extra socks or clothing.

The Ranking System (1-10)

The numeric number on the top of each entry indicates the overall rating of the swimming hole. The author considered various systems for ranking the various swimming holes. It becomes quite evident that all swimming holes are not created equal and some are better than others. Further, how one determines better can be somewhat subjective. However, swimming hole aficionados will appreciate a numeric ranking system since it helps to make fine distinctions between the various swimming holes. In this book the rankings are on a scale of from 1 to 10 with 1 being the lowest ranking and 10 being the highest ranking. For point of reference a city beach gets a "1" ranking.

There are no swimming holes in this book that score below a "4" on this ranking system. There are a number of important sub-criteria that can be used in rating a swimming hole. For purposes of this book the following criteria were considered in the rankings: the quality and beauty of the location, the nature and style of the cliffs and rock formations, the presence of tubs, a waterfall or rock water slide, the length of the hike, the quality of the roads getting to the site, the temperature, depth, and quality of the water, the presence of a vertical (rocks for jumping) and horizontal component (beach, sand, trees etc.), the privacy afforded by the site, the presence or absence of dams or man-made obstructions, the proximity of services such as gas stations, restaurants, and bathrooms, and the presence or existence of slabs or rocks for sunbathing.

Etiquette & Ethics

There are a number of important etiquette and ethics considerations when hiking to swimming holes. Some of the considerations are self-evident, like staying together in a group, allowing fast people on the trail to pass, and packing out your litter and waste. Others might not be so obvious like not cutting switchbacks, or being at least 200 yards away from the river when urinating.

The author is also familiar with a number of swimming holes whose rocks have been subject to vandalism like graffiti. These swimming holes are generally within a mile or less to the trailhead.

In the event that you notice graffiti or the vandals in progress, you should immediately report it to the forest ranger station.

Shasta & Trinity

★ HATCHET CREEK FALLS

Shasta-Trinity National Forest off of Hwy. 299 near Redding
Access: Hike 0.25 miles one way (0.5 miles round trip)
Elevation: Starts at 1800 feet, total gain of 50 feet
Level: Easy

Bathrooms nearby: No
Water Temperature: Moderate
Clothing Optional: No
Dog/Kid friendly: Yes
Best Season: July–September, Year-round for Waterfall viewing

Hatchet Creek Falls is located near the isolated "town" of Big Bend, which is itself located on the banks of the Pit River. Locals refer to the falls as "Hatchet Creek Falls," but USGS maps identify it as "Lion Slide Falls." The falls is most easily identified by the large fir tree that has toppled over its lip and bisects the cataract. The swimming hole is fantastic.

Hatchet Creek features a large, round, 40-foot-deep pool at its base. The falls are quite strong all year round and make it difficult to swim directly up to the area right under the falls. The falls are about 25 feet high and about 30 feet wide during high flow periods.

Steps have been cut into the fir tree to ascend and jump from into the large pool below.

The temperature of the swimming hole is moderate, but drops a few degrees if you swim closer to the falls. There are a number of beach spaces for pulling up lawn chairs with a cooler to watch the action. Boy is there diving action! On more than one occasion the author has watched as diving acrobats appear to attempt the impossible.

This is a very popular place with teenagers and locals that come up from the Indian Reservation. Cliff jumping and diving is quite popular from all areas around the falls.

Although the pool is shallow near its edges, it does get quite deep out near the falls. The pool depth is around 10 feet in most places and probably double that closer to the falls. No one really just stumbles onto Hatchet Creek Falls. It's known by most of the locals and they are willing to drive from areas as far as Shasta and Redding. It's considered one of the best swimming holes in all of the Shasta and Redding areas.

Getting to Hatchet Creek Falls is actually quite easy. You simply follow the highway and then come to a turn off on the right. There is usually plenty of parking, but the place is usually identified by the other cars parked on the side of the road. The trail to the falls is at the back right side of the parking area. From there you just follow the trail up for about 200 yards to the swimming area. The trail will go steeply up to the right. You actually want to go down closer to the river and walk as far up the right bank as you can. Be careful because it can get slippery. You will reach a point that you can't go any further without wading into the water. From there you should be able to find a spot to relax and pull up a chair.

The pool at the base of the falls is crystal clear and stays that way because it's continually refreshed by the flow of the falls. On a hot summer day you will find it difficult to pull yourself out of the water to go home. All around a great swimming hole with excellent vertical and horizontal components.

Restaurant and Bathrooms:

The closest bathrooms and restaurants are in Big Bend.

Information and Contact:

There is no fee here. For a map of Shasta-Trinity National Forest, please visit the website www.fs.fed.us/r5/maps/. For additional information contact Shasta-Trinity National Forest,

Shasta Lake Ranger District, 14225 Holiday Rd., Redding, CA 96003, 530/275-1587.

For additional photos and a video, please visit our website at:

http://swimmingholesofcalifornia.blogspot.com

Highlights:

If you like jumping from cliffs and don't like to hike, this is the place for you. A great place to stop if you are heading to Mt. Shasta or McArthur Burney Falls.

Driving Directions:

From Redding, take Hwy. 299 east for about 35 miles. The road meanders along the river for quite some time and then ascends up the side of a mountain. Continue on this road until you reach Big Bend Rd. on the left. Take a left on Big Bend Rd. and drive about 0.8 miles until you reach the bridge over Hatchet Creek. You should park in the dirt parking area at the right. The unmarked trail begins at the back of the parking area on the right side.

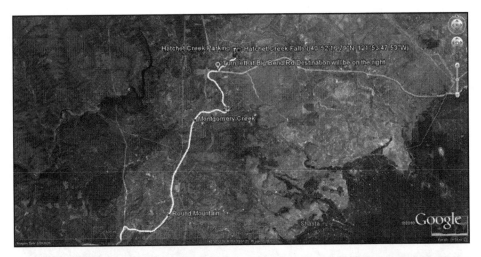

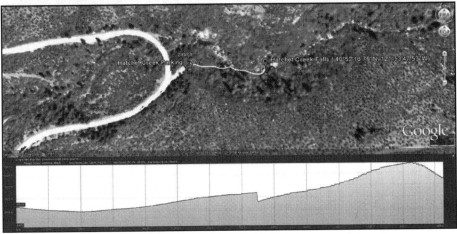

★7 McCLOUD FALLS

Shasta-Trinity National Forest, off of Hwy. 89 near
McCloud
Access: Hike 0.5 miles one way (1.0 miles round trip)
Elevation: Starts at 3050 feet, total gain 600 ft
Level: Easy

Bathrooms nearby: Yes
Water Temperature: Moderate
Clothing Optional: No
Dog/Kid friendly: Yes
Best Season: April – September

Three big and beautiful waterfalls and swimming holes all ready for the taking. McCloud Falls has almost something for everyone. Contrary to what most of the guide books tell you, all of these falls are capable of easy drive-up by automobile. The easy approach somewhat lowers the expectation of privacy. However, who cares because the falls are just so beautiful!

Each of the falls is distinct in character. The upper falls requires a little work to get down to. There is a nice viewing area just above the falls. A large and narrow shoot of about 90 feet in length steps down in five steps (two steps are viewable) to feed an enormous 100-foot diameter hole. In the spring and during high flow rates the water shoots out of the gorgeous narrow rock gorge like an uncapped fire hydrant or broken pipe. However, this water is clean and aquamarine in color.

The middle falls is the most spectacular of them all. It boasts a height of around 81 feet and a whopping width of around 100 feet The most interesting part of the falls is how the river has carved the stone at such a steep angle that the water falls almost directly downward.

This makes the pool below ideal for swimming. The falls look more like a curtain draped over a large oval pool filled with dark green and aquamarine water. It's a pure joy. The left wall of the middle falls is fairly steep basalt rock. Many swimmers like to scale the walls to dive or reach the top of the falls for jumping. The right side of the falls comprises plants, stones, and Elephant Ears. This gives the falls a slight tropical feeling, as if one has just entered a secret paradise.

The lower falls is a busy family swimming hole complete with viewing area, platform, and metal ladder to assist swimmers and jumpers that enter the oval pool below the falls. The falls are about 12 feet high and feed a large round pool of about 60 feet or more in diameter.

Each of the falls is joined by a hiking trail that you can pick up just below Fowlers Campground at the lower falls. There are parking lots at each of the falls with bathrooms. The expectation of privacy is fair at McCloud Falls. The most heavily used swimming hole is the lower falls, followed by the middle falls, and then the upper falls.

If you visit the Shasta area, no trip would be complete without stopping by at McCloud Falls. As in the movie *Highlander* with Duncan & Connor MacLeod (spelled differently), one should pay homage to each of the falls. Further, this grand set of swimming holes will forever make an immortal impression on you. As in the movie *Highlander*, "the gathering" is referred to as a reunion that the last few immortals meet and fight each other until one is left. So with McCloud Falls, you will "gather" with friends and sample each falls until you decide which one is the best. It happens all the time. For in the end, given limited time, there can be only one swimming hole.

Restaurant and Bathrooms:

There are bathrooms at each of the parking lots and falls. Closest restaurants are in the town of Shasta or McCloud.

Information and Contact:

There is no fee here. For a map of the Shasta-Trinity Forest, contact the office below or visit the website at www.fs.fed.us/r5/maps/. For more information, contact Shasta-Trinity National Forest, McCloud Ranger District, P.O. Box 1620, 2019 Forest Rd., McCloud, CA 96057, 530/964-2184, website: www.fs.fed.us/r5/shastatrinity.

For additional photos and to view a creative video of the three falls, please visit our website at:

http://swimmingholesofcalifornia.blogspot.com

Highlights

You can take the kids and grandparents to the swimming area at the lower falls. Some areas allow fishing and kayaking. On the drive up, don't forget to stop at McArthur Burney Falls off of Hwy. 89 near Burney. They are a spectacular drive up falls. There is a fee though to enter the park.

MCCLOUD FALLS

MCCLOUD FALLS

Driving Directions:

From Redding, drive north on Interstate 5 for about 2 miles until you reaching the exit for Hwy. 299. Take Hwy. 299 east as it winds along the river for about 47 miles. Stop at Burney Falls if desired. Drive another 10 miles until you reach the Hwy. 89 exit. Bear Left on Hwy. 89 and drive 30 miles until the Fowler Campground (it will be on the left-hand side). If you miss the turn off you will drive directly into the town of McCloud. Take the exit into the Fowler Campground and drive about 1.0 miles to the lower falls (stay right all the way). At the last fork the road to the left leads to the middle and upper falls. You will know you are on the correct road because of the pot holes that are present all over the road.

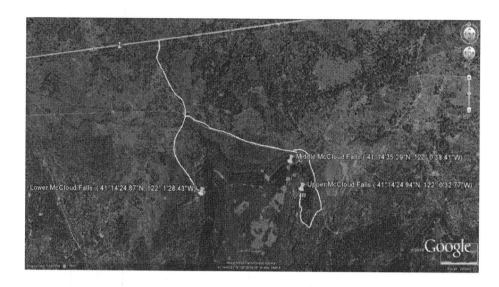

★4 NORTH FORK TRINITY RIVER & PARADISE POOLS

Shasta & Trinity Alps Wilderness Area, near Helena off of Hwy. 299
Access: Hike or bike 0.5 miles round trip
Level: Easy to Moderate

Bathrooms nearby: Yes
Water Temperature: Cold
Clothing Optional: No
Dog/Kid friendly: Yes
Best Season: Good to visit all year round

Here's a place to visit if you are in the area. The North Fork of the Trinity River and Paradise Pools provide ample opportunity for just about everything you could want in a swimming hole. Getting there though can take some time. It's basically located outside of Redding and Whiskey Lake. Just keep driving until you reach Weaverville and then drive some more until you reach the town of Helena. The reality is there is no town of Helena. It's a ghost town with nothing more than a few interesting buildings on East Forks Rd.

Depending upon the time of year that you visit will dictate which swimming hole you visit. The water is both cold and a beautiful emerald green color. This area is great for fishing, bird watching, and viewing wild life. If you visit early in the spring chances are you will have it all to yourself. It's about 0.5 miles to reach the first swimming hole. It's a bend in the river with a great 8-foot jumping rock and oval hole that is about 12 feet deep. There is also a nice rope swing across the river.

If you visit later in the year, or in the summer, you may have to move further up the river to Paradise Pools to obtain some privacy. Paradise Pools is located another 0.2 miles up the road. You simply cross the bridge and look for the trail to the right of the river.

The trail runs adjacent to the river. It's not in very good shape, and in some cases it may just be as easy to swim or walk up the river. The first hole you will reach is oval, about 20 feet deep, and provides good vertical and horizontal elements. The horizontal element includes a number of good rocks for sunbathing and some rock "butt buckets" for sitting by the river. Further up is a 15-foot jump that allows plunges into "Little Paradise."

Still further up the river is another swimming hole with even a higher cliff for jumping that is likely to be 75 feet or higher. Extreme care should be taken when jumping here since the "sweet spot" is fairly small. The locals referred to this as "Credential." Essentially you graduate to the Hall of Fame if you make the jump and come back alive.

These swimming holes are a great place to meet people. The locals here are really friendly and willing to direct you to wherever you want to go.

Restaurant and Bathrooms:

There are bathrooms up the road in Weaverville, California.

Information and Contact:

There is no fee here.

Highlights

There is some great fishing in the area. Further, a number of Bald Eagles and other wild life can be spotted around the river. If you plan to stop in Redding, you might want to consider having lunch or dinner at the Moonstone Bistro. Try the "Fresh Catch." It's to die for! There are a number of great hikes nearby including the Canyon Creek Trail and Grizzly Lake hike.

NORTH FORK TRINITY RIVER & PARADISE POOLS

NORTH FORK TRINITY RIVER & PARADISE POOLS

Driving Directions:

From Redding take State Route 299 West 58.3 miles to East Forks Rd. (CR 412). Drive north on the road (only one direction possible) for less than 0.5 miles to the abandoned town of Helena, California. The first swimming hole is less than 0.5 miles on the right. There is a dirt parking area and a large rock in the river can be easily spotted. For Paradise Pools continue further north on East Forks Rd. until you reach the bridge. Park on the North West side of the bridge and boulder hop and cliff climb for about 10 minutes until you reach "Little Paradise." Keep going up the river for another 10 minutes to reach "Big Paradise" or "Credential."

POTEM FALLS

Shasta-Trinity National Forest, off of Hwy. 299 near Redding

Access: Hike 0.25 miles one way (0.5 miles round trip)

Elevation: Starts at 1800 feet; total loss of 50 feet

Level: Easy

Bathrooms nearby: No

Water Temperature: Moderate

Clothing Optional: Yes

Dog/Kid friendly: No

Best Season: Good to visit all year round

Potem falls is one of those places that are so spectacular you want to keep it to yourself. The falls is about 70 feet high and plunges over a rock cliff into a perfect circular pool below. It's located at the bottom of a small canyon that is lined with oak trees, and all types of beautiful plant vegetation. The falls give you the feeling of being in an enclosed room. Further, given the steep drop of the falls combined with the generous plant life one could easily be confused and think that you are in Hawaii. Potem Falls is paradise on earth. The water is not too cold and there is both a generous vertical and horizontal element. Care should be taken though not to climb to the top of the falls, because there have been a number of injuries.

There is a small rope swing and a number of flat rocks to lay out on at the left side of the swimming hole closest to the falls. There is also ample space near the trail and to the right of the falls. The water depth is at least 10 feet at the base of the falls.

Most people who venture to Potem Falls are locals who regard it as a secret swimming hole. To get there requires a drive on unpaved road for about 6 miles. The road is easily passable by most passenger vehicles. You will know you are on the right track when you reach the bridge that crosses the Pitt River.

It's a fairly narrow bridge. Once you cross the bridge the road becomes worse in condition. The good news is you only have about 0.25 miles left to drive. The trailhead to the falls is marked by a large concrete block near the pullout on the left.

The trail down to the falls is fairly steep. There are a number of large switchbacks you need to descend until you reach the base of the falls. The privacy here is excellent. The water temperature is also reasonable year-round because the water derives from Lake Shasta and not from snow or glacier runoff.

Restaurant and Bathrooms:

The closest bathrooms are at the area just under the bridge that crosses the Pitt River.

Information and Contact:

There is no fee here.

For additional photos, please visit our website at:

http://swimmingholesofcalifornia.blogspot.com

Highlights

You can take the kids to the swimming area just under the bridge over the Pitt River.

Bring a blanket and picnic basket and spend the day with that special person watching the falls.

POTEM FALLS

Driving Directions:

From Redding, take Hwy. 299 East and drive 29 miles. Turn left on Fenders Ferry Rd. and drive 9 miles (the pavement ends at 3.5 miles and the road turns to dirt). Look for a large unmarked parking pullout and cement block that mark the start of the trail. You can hear the falls from the road. High clearance vehicles are recommended, but not required.

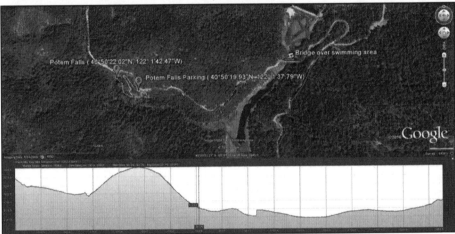

6 **SHACKLEFORD FALLS**

Klamath National Forest off of Hwy. 3 near Fort Jones

Access: Hike 0.25 miles one way (0.5 miles round trip)

Elevation: Starts at 2400 feet; total gain of 0 feet

Level: Easy

Bathrooms nearby: No

Water Temperature: Moderate

Clothing Optional: No

Dog/Kid friendly: Yes

Best Season: June–September, year-round for waterfall viewing

Shackleford Falls is one of those swimming holes that you don't just wonder off and find. It's in a remote part of California near the border of Oregon. So that's the bad news. The good news is that it's a great swimming hole only really used by locals. For this reason, much of the time you can have the place all to yourself.

The falls run almost year round. They are great to visit at almost any time. The best swimming months are going to be July and August. If you want to visit the falls when they are really running then visit them in the months of March and April.

A 20-foot waterfall drops down through a narrow constriction into a small rocky gorge. The waterfall creates an enclosed oblong swimming hole that is roughly 20 to 30 feet wide in diameter. The falls drops down at an angle that is essentially orthogonal to the stream that flows from the swimming hole.

There are both good vertical and horizontal elements. There are many different rocks to relax and watch the falls. The vertical element comprises a number of small cliffs for jumping. The highest cliff being about 35 feet directly opposite the falls. The depth of the swimming hole is hard to judge, but looks to be about 10 to 12 feet. Depth can vary during the year due to varying flow rates.

The falls is actually located on private property owned by the Fruit Growers Supply Company. However, they generally allow people to use the swimming hole and falls.

The pool at the base of the falls is crystal clear and stays that way because it's continually refreshed by the flow of the falls. On a hot summer day you will find it difficult to pull yourself out of the water to go home.

Restaurant and Bathrooms:

The closet bathrooms and restaurants are in Fort Jones.

Information and Contact:

There is no fee here. For a map of Klamath National Forest, please visit the website www.fs.fed.us/r5/maps/. For additional information contact: Klamath National Forest, Scott and Salmon River Ranger District, 11263 N. Hwy. 3, Fort Jones, CA 96032, 530/468-535, website: www.fs.fed.us/r5/klamath.

Highlights

If you like jumping from cliffs and don't like to hike, this is the place for you. A great place to stop if you are heading to Crater Lake or Mt. Shasta.

SHACKLEFORD FALLS

Driving Directions:

From I-5 at Yreka, take Hwy. 3 exit and drive west for about 16.5 miles to Fort Jones. Turn right on Scott River Rd. and drive 7 miles, then take the left fork. The fork is easy to miss so keep a lookout for it. The road you are turning onto is called Quartz Valley Rd. Drive 3.9 miles on Quartz Valley Rd. and turn right on Rd. 43N21. There is a small sign that is not so easy to read. However, it does say Shackleford Falls clearly. Drive 1.2 miles on 43N21, until you reach the first bridge. The road is dirt, but is in fairly good condition. The bridge is fairly obvious given that it has a small guardrail. You can park on both sides of the bridge. The trailhead is located on the further side of the bridge. This would be roughly the right side of the bridge and river as you look upstream.

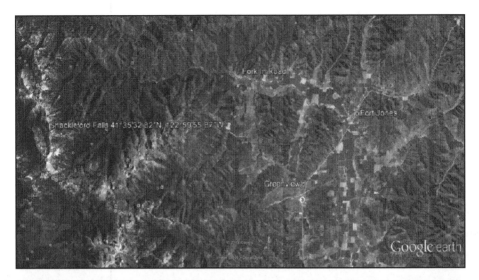

HUMBOLDT, MENDOCINO & THE REDWOODS

GOAT ROCK

Humboldt County, Near Grizzly Creek Redwood State Park
Access: Hike 0.25 miles one way (05 miles round trip)
Level: Easy

Bathrooms nearby: Yes, at the state park entrance
Water Temperature: Moderate/warm
Clothing Optional: No
Dog/Kid friendly: No
Best Season: July & August
Note: Trail is not easy to find and descent is steep to the river

Goat Rock has been referred to by some as an enchanting paradise. It has everything one could want from a swimming hole. It has a sandy beach, privacy, beautiful clean aquamarine water, and its own small falls. All of this is tucked beneath a towering outcrop of stone and earth hundreds of feet high and heavily forested all the way down to the river. About the only thing Goat Rock does not have is a good vertical element or place for jumping. However, why complain with such a great beach and privacy?

Goat Rock is a swimming hole that is fairly easy to reach, but not easy to find. This would explain why it has its own privacy element. The small falls feeds into an elbow in the river that is lined by beautiful Elephant Ears and other plants. The swimming hole is about 8 to 10 feet deep. Finding the trail down to the base of Goat Rock is not as easy as one would think.

From the road you can actually see the monolith. However, no trails down can be seen anywhere. The trail is actually located between highway marker 2258 and 2256.

A giant concrete block has been placed directly in the trail entrance blocking the access. A number of people simply made a trail around the block. Given that the trail no longer gets very heavy use it has become somewhat overgrown at the entrance point. After you break through some of the brush and follow the trail it gets better. It isn't until near the end of the trail that it gets steep requiring less nimble hikers to slide down a portion of the trail to get down a small rock precipice.

Restaurant and Bathrooms:

The closest bathrooms are at the Grizzly Creek Redwood State Park just up the road.

Information and Contact:

There is no fee to enter this area.

Highlights

There are a number of other swimming holes in the area. Plan ahead and also visit some of the Big Trees.

GOAT ROCK

GOAT ROCK

Driving Directions:

From U.S. 101 drive exactly 20.7 miles east on Route 36 to Golden Gate Park Dr. on the right, which is two miles west of Bridgeville (or drive 7.0 miles east of Grizzly Creek State Park). Look for mile marker 2258. Drive exactly 1.0 miles farther east to a turnout opposite the massive Goat Rock monolith above the river. Take the narrow river access trail down 130 yards to the river. There is a large cement block blocking the access way. The trail is overgrown, but gets better. The trail gets steeper at the bottom.

HOLMES FLAT BAR

Humboldt County, Humboldt Redwood State Park
Access: No hike
Level: Easy

Bathrooms nearby: Yes, along the Avenue of the Giants
Water Temperature: Moderate/warm
Clothing Optional: No
Dog/Kid friendly: Yes
Best Season: May-August
Note: Parking lot takes you to the flat and beach

Holmes Flat Bar requires no hike. Surprised? It's an ideal place to stop if you are in a hurry to visit the Avenue of the Giants and want to take a quick dip and don't mind sharing the beach with your friends, family, and the locals. This is a beautiful one-mile stretch of sandy beach on the Eel River. With so much great sand, it's hard to believe that it's not salt water you are swimming in. You can drive down the dry wash and cross to many popular swimming holes. The swimming hole is deepest on the northeast side closest to the majestic sandstone bluffs.

Contrary to what most people might believe as you go further north from San Francisco, the water in most of the swimming holes actually becomes warmer. Some of the best water temperatures are in the swimming holes in Humboldt County. Holmes flat bar is no exception. This swimming hole is great for families, small groups, older people, and even children.

Restaurant and Bathrooms:

The closest bathrooms are just off of the Avenue of the Giants.

Information and Contact:

There is no fee to enter this area.

Highlights

There are a number of other swimming holes in the area. Plan ahead and also visit some of the big trees or even places where portions of famous movies were photographed (like *Star Wars*).

HOLMES FLAT BAR

Driving Directions:

Take the Holmes-Redcrest exit 667 and go north (take a left) onto the Avenue of the Giants. Go 1.3 miles to the Holmes turnoff on the right. Then go 1.3 miles to the "T" in the road. Turn left at the "T" and drive 1/3 mile to the end of the road. Drive down the dry wash and park.

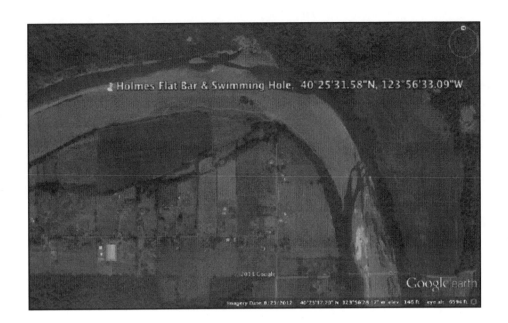

CHICO, PLUMAS & THE FEATHER RIVER

★ 6   BEAR HOLE

Chico, California, just outside of Redding (Upper Bidwell Park)
Access: Hike 0.25 miles one way (0.5 miles round trip)
Level: Easy

Bathrooms nearby: Yes
Water Temperature: Moderate
Clothing Optional: No
Dog/Kid friendly: Yes
Best Season: Good to visit all year round

This swimming hole gets the prize for the best rock formations. Bear Hole is a favorite for many of the locals from Chico, California. You will see lots of younger people from Chico State also. The black lava rock you see all around the swimming hole is basalt. It's a type of lava rock formed by rapid cooling of Lovejoy basalt. It's very rare indeed to have such rocks at a swimming hole.

Bear Hole is a part of Big Chico Creek in Upper Bidwell Park. It's used as a swimming Hole, as the water is especially deep here in the late spring and summer. Diving off of the high rocks is a popular activity at Bear Hole, but swimmers should be aware that this is incredibly dangerous and can lead to serious injuries that could be deadly. Additionally, the water currents can move quickly through the area, so swimmers should be careful to not get caught in faster moving waters that could trap them.

The water is deep enough in the central pool to jump off the lower rocks with a three to five-foot drop. The basalt cliffs that line Bear Hole rise about 30 feet above the water, providing enough rock to admire without feeling enclosed or claustrophobic. In addition to swimming, sunbathing is popular at Bear Hole.

Bear Hole is a great swimming hole for children who are decent swimmers and capable of climbing down the pathway themselves. Like all the sites listed here, it's also well suited for adults and college students alike; just be sure to always swim with a buddy and keep a sharp eye on the kids.

Further up past Bear Hole is Diversion Dam. Many people like to use this area for jumping. Although the author would say that the "sweet spot" is quite narrow.

As one proceeds still further up the Canyon toward Salmon Hole and Brown's hole there are more clothing optional opportunities. Salmon hole has a rope swing, deep, round, 60-foot pool, and the highest cliffs for jumping at around 50 feet.

As a part of Bidwell Park, all park rules apply, including the alcohol ban and the glass ban.

Restaurant and Bathrooms:

The closest bathrooms are in Bidwell Park. There are some good restaurants in Chico, California.

Information and Contact:

There is no fee to enter this area and park.

For additional photos and a video, please visit our website at:

http://swimmingholesofcalifornia.blogspot.com

Highlights

This can be a popular place. There are a number of places to swim. The water temperature is moderate. There are a number of underwater caves to swim through.

BEAR HOLE

BEAR HOLE

Driving Directions:

From Chico, at the intersection of East Ave and State Rt. 99, go east on East Ave. for 2.7 miles to Manzanita Ave. and continue east a few hundred feet before turning onto Manzanita Ave. Next continue east a couple of hundred feet before turning left on Wildwood Rd. Follow Wildwood Rd. 2 miles into Bidwell Park. Follow the signs to Big Chico Creek and Bear Hole.

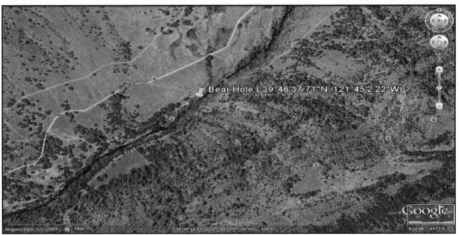

DRY CREEK

Spencerville Wildlife Area, off of Hwy. 20 near Marysville

Access: Hike or bike 5.0 miles round trip

Level: Easy to Moderate

Bathrooms nearby: No

Water Temperature: Moderate to cold

Clothing Optional: No

Dog/Kid friendly: Yes

Best Season: Good to visit all year round

Dry Creek is one of those special swimming holes that you can visit all year round. There is nothing particularly dry about Dry Creek since it's supplied by a perennial spring that feeds the falls and the swimming hole all year round. So Dry Creek like Carlon Falls is one of the few swimming holes you can visit even late in the Fall season.

If there is an award for being the most colorful swimming hole, it would probably go to Dry Creek. Various colors are supplied by the rocks, cliffs, water, and surrounding vegetation. Another misunderstanding concerns the large size of the falls and the swimming hole at its base. The falls is fairly large and the pool it feeds into is massive. However, almost all photos of the falls appear to make the falls and pool look fairly small. We were presently surprised to realize the falls was quite substantial. It would appear to be approximately 50 feet high and the pool at its base at least 50 yards across. The water drops off the cliff and hits a ledge, changes direction and then free falls again. It's quite rewarding and relaxing to watch.

The swimming hole is actually quite deep. The depth was hard to judge given the dark color of the water. However, we would guess deeper than 30 feet in places. Given the steep cliffs and deep pool, the vertical element here is quite good. Further, across from the falls are a number of rocks and flat stones that provide a great horizontal element.

It's remarkable that the expectation of privacy here also appears to be quite good. We've rated the hike to be easy to moderate. After hiking the trails on more than one occasion, there does appear to be an elevation gain that is substantial, but not easy to notice given the gentle and consistent grade. Further, it's not clear that the distance reported is accurate. Perhaps the hike distance is slightly longer than reported. Last, you will reach a point on the hike in which the trail forks. You have a choice to go up further into the hills or stay lower closer to the river. In our opinion, the route that goes up into the hills is the shortest, most scenic, and best route to the falls.

Restaurant and Bathrooms:

There are bathrooms up the road at some local gas stations and stores.

Information and Contact:

There is no fee here.

For additional photos, please visit our website at:

http://swimmingholesofcalifornia.blogspot.com

Highlights

From time to time Wild Turkeys have been seen on the property. Further, there is a donkey farm nearby that breeds miniature donkeys.

DRY CREEK

DRY CREEK

Driving Directions:

From Marysville, drive east on Hwy. 20 for approximately 14 miles, then turn right (south) on Smartville Rd. Drive 0.9 miles and bear left at the fork to stay on Smartville Rd. Continue another 3.8 miles to Waldo Rd. and bear left on the gravel road. Follow Waldo Rd. 1.9 miles to the Waldo Bridge. Cross the bridge and turn left on Spencerville Rd. Drive 2.2 miles to the end of the road at an old, blocked-off bridge. Park in the parking lot and cross over the bridge. Note: from Grass Valley, the drive is 12.5 miles west on Hwy. 20 to Smartville Rd., then turn left (south and continue as above).

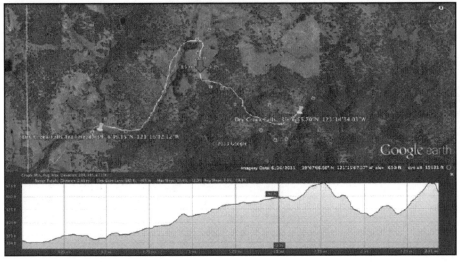

★ 8 FEATHER FALLS

Plumas National Forest off of Hwy. 70 near Orville
Access: Hike 7.4-9.8 miles round trip
Elevation: Starts at 2,400 feet; total gain 1000 ft
Level: Difficult

Bathrooms nearby: Yes at trailhead parking lot
Water Temperature: Moderate
Clothing Optional: Depends the time of year
Dog/Kid friendly: No, steep and long hike
Best Season: July-September (swimming), hiking all year round

Feather Falls is one of the highest falls in California. It has a pedigree and is the sixth highest falls in the United States. It drops 640 feet and then continues for another half mile down to the Middle Fork of the Feather River, which is damned near Lake Orville. We rated this swimming hole an "8." The falls are generally rated a "10" out of "10" in most books. We rate the swimming holes a "5," but combined with the plant life, second swimming hole on the long loop trail, view, and falls, the overall rating is around an "8."

Most people don't really think of Feather Falls as a swimming hole place. It's all about the falls and the hike to get there. However, given that the temperatures get scorching hot in this canyon, you will find even the simplest swimming holes here quite refreshing. Further, the swimming hole is very easy to get to and not too far from the overlook platform (about

0.25 miles maximum). The swimming hole is close to the top of the falls. However, given the way the drainage works most times of the year it flows fairly calm even at the lip of the falls. It's a nice place to relax, submerge oneself and enjoy the beautiful Elephant Ears and other plant life. There is no vertical or horizontal element though (rocks for jumping or beach).

There are two trails to get to the falls. The trail is a loop; one side is short and steep and the other side is more gradual, but longer in distance. There is much debate what is the best way to hike to Feather Falls. We definitely recommend the short route (down) and the longer more gradual route back. That makes for a 9.8-mile hike. There is also a second place to swim and dunk oneself under the falls on the longer route back. This makes for the perfect hike. If you go up and down the short route the hike is about 7.4 miles. The hike up is a real challenge.

In the summer, this has to be one of the hottest canyons in California. Pack extra water for sure. You might also want to bring along a bug repellant if you hike later in the summer or fall. Although not a high theft area, please make sure to secure all valuables prior to leaving your car.

Restaurant and Bathrooms:

There is a general store in Orville to stock up. There are restrooms at the trailhead parking lot.

Information and Contact:

There is no fee. For a map of Plumas National Forest, please contact the office or visit the website at www.fs.fed.us/r5/maps/. For more information, please contact the Plumas National Forest, Feather River Ranger District, 875 Mitchell Ave., Oroville, CA 95965, 530/534-6500, website: www.fs.fed. us/r5/plumas.

For photos of the falls please visit our website at:

http://swimmingholesofcalifornia.blogspot.com

Highlights

This can be a popular place. Another great swimming hole in the area is Seven Falls.

FEATHER FALLS

FEATHER FALLS

Driving Directions:

From Hwy. 70 in Oroville, take the Oroville Dam Blvd. exit (Hwy. 162 east) and drive 1.6 miles to Olive Hwy./Hwy. 162. Turn right on Forbes Town Rd. and drive six miles. Turn left on Lumpkin Rd. and drive 10.8 miles. Turn left at the sign and look for the sign for Feather Falls. Drive 1.6 miles to the trailhead.

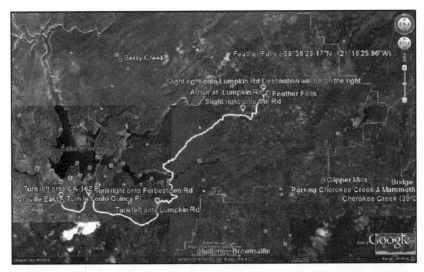

LITTLE NORTH FORK

Plumas National Forest, off of Forest Service 119
(Brush Creek Ranger Station)
Access: Hike 20 yards off of FS60
Elevation: Total loss of 30 feet
Level: Easy

Bathrooms nearby: No
Water Temperature: Moderate
Clothing Optional: Yes
Dog/Kid friendly: Yes
Best Season: July & August
Note: 9 miles of rough road

Little North Fork is a special type of swimming hole. It was really designed for campers. Little North Fork Campground is only about 0.25 miles or less away just across a small bridge. So campers take note. This is your swimming hole! Further, if you stay at the Little North Fork Campground, chances are you may have this swimming hole all to yourself. The privacy is somewhat diminished due to the swimming hole being right off of Forest Service 60. If you camp at Little North Fork you can get up early in the morning and go for an early morning swim dressed in your best birthday suit.

The trail down to the swimming hole is right near a large alder tree. The trail is a little steep and you won't even notice the swimming hole until you are right on top of it. In order to appreciate this swimming hole you need to be down in it.

If this swimming hole didn't already have a name, it would more appropriately be named "The Abyss." There is a large rock impound that forms the swimming hole. The rock impound drops off like a ledge forming a deep and mysterious hole. This is a very deep swimming hole to say the least.

Further down there are a couple of other swimming holes that are not as deep, but provide additional privacy. The vertical and horizontal elements are pretty good, but nothing special.

Overall, a decent swimming hole, but not a place to drive to and spend just one day. You will have about 9 miles of crappy road to drive on. Campers and regular cars can make the trip, but they will need to take it slow. By the way, don't even try to drive through or to pass beyond Little North Fork Campground. The road just gets worse and steeper and it's very easy to get lost. You will know when you reach the Little North Fork Campground because you will drive over a bridge and guardrail, and Little North Fork Campground will be on your left hand side. The road then proceeds up.

Restaurant and Bathrooms:

The closest bathrooms are at the Brush Creek Ranger Station.

Information and Contact:

There is no fee here.

For additional photos, please visit our website at:

http://swimmingholesofcalifornia.blogspot.com

Highlights

Camp overnight and have the swimming hole all to yourself!

LITTLE NORTH FORK

Driving Directions:

From Oroville, take Route 162 north 26 miles to the Brush Creek Ranger Station in Plumas National Forest. Follow FS 119 to FS 60. It will be at an intersection and will be to the right. Follow FS 60 for about 9 miles. The road will quickly change to gravel and then dirt. You will cross over a paved bridge with guardrails. The road will continue for quite some time and will not be close to the river. The swimming hole will be on the right just before you cross a small bridge with metal guardrails. If you continue on you will drive almost directly into the Little North Fork Campground that will be on your left hand side. Four-wheel drive is recommended, but not required.

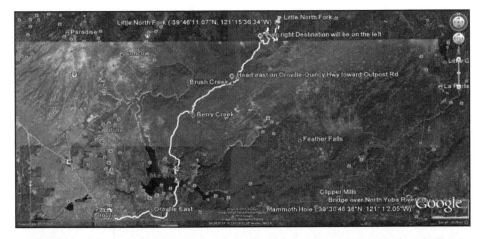

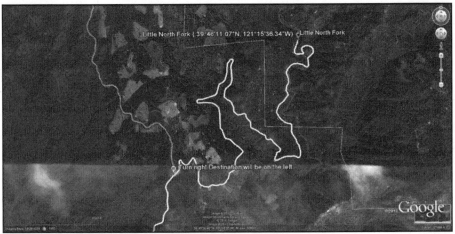

ROCK CREEK

Plumas National Forest (near Oroville, CA)
Access: Hike 0.25 miles one way (05 mile round trip)
Level: Easy

Bathrooms nearby: Yes
Water Temperature: Moderate
Clothing Optional: Yes, upper holes
Dog/Kid friendly: No
Best Season: July & August

Rock Creek is a waterpark of Olympian beauty. It has just about everything to make it the perfect swimming hole. There are rocks for jumping into the main pool, there is a great area under the trees for having a picnic, and there is the waterslide. When we say "the water slide," we mean "the water slide"! This slide is run all year round at no admission price, no crowds, and unlimited sliding possibilities. You can slide on your backside, or earlier in the year bring your own flotation device and go for it!

The water at Rock Creek is moderate in temperature and has a beautiful emerald color. There are also a number of trees around the creek which provide just the right amount of shade to make the place the ideal temperature and not too sunny even on the hottest days. Just below Rock Creek is another swimming hole with a small 20-foot falls. Various boulders in the middle, but still deep enough for swimming.

Above Rock Creek is another beautiful set of falls. The falls are separated by a large rock. There are a number of small clothing optional tubs. There is a small passageway just under the large rock to allow access to still another swimming hole that is about 15 feet deep. The walls on both sides are about 75 feet high. This swimming hole is almost never used. For this reason, we regard it as clothing optional and the expectation of privacy would be considered great. When using the waterslide it's easiest to exit on the left side of the creek (when looking upstream).

Restaurant and Bathrooms:

There are bathrooms right at the parking lot. The closest gas station and restaurants are in Oroville, California.

Information and Contact:

There is no fee here.

For additional photos, please visit our website at:

http://swimmingholesofcalifornia.blogspot.com

Highlights

Little North Fork and Milsap Campground are nearby.

ROCK CREEK

ROCK CREEK

Driving Directions:

Continue on Rt. 70 along the Feather River (as above) and go about 1 mile past the Cresta Dam to the area where Rock Creek comes in from the north to join the Feather River. There are several swimming holes near here. To get to the first, park at the first wide spot and scramble upstream (not much of a trail) on the right side of Rock Creek for about 20 minutes to a small waterfall and swimming hole. For another, easier to get to, drive about another .5 miles to another parking spot and walk north about .25 miles along an old road to where there is a water slide into a large pool and a number of other smaller holes nearby. If you continue to walk upstream from here, on the left bank, and squeeze between some boulders, there is yet another hole.

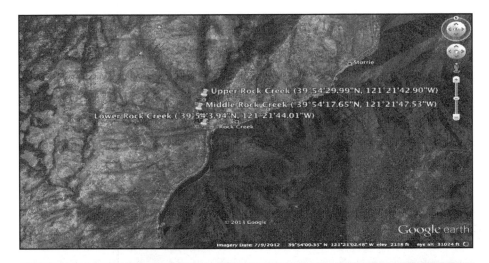

SEVEN FALLS

Plumas National Forest off of Hwy. 70 near Orville
Access: Steep 1.0 miles hike
Elevation: Starts at 2,300 feet; total loss 1500 ft
Level: Difficult

Bathrooms nearby: No
Water Temperature: Cold
Clothing Optional: Yes
Dog/Kid friendly: No, steep and difficult hike
Best Season: July-September (swimming) Hiking all year round

No swimming hole book would be complete without a reference to Seven Falls. Seven Falls is the Shangri-La of swimming holes. The place it not easy to access and is quite hidden and its location is kept secret by many. The hike to Seven Falls is quite strenuous. There are places on the trail that require some careful footing. The water is also cold during most of the year.

It's highly likely that you will have the swimming hole completely to yourself. It should be noted that you do not want to visit Seven Falls too early in the year. The water and falls can be quite strong in early spring. After a few months when the water levels subside, the river becomes much more hospitable.

The featured swimming hole is actually at the third falls. Extreme caution should be exercised when trying to climb above or below this falls given the steep granite, cliffs, and loose scree.

The main problem with Seven Falls is the road getting there. The road really requires four-wheel drive. The best approach is to drive down Milsap Bar Rd. The approach from below is much more difficult and slow going. So take our word for it, come in from the top and you will be fine. Most of the road is fairly tame except for the last 1/4 mile that requires some slower driving.

Seven Falls has it all, great big waterfalls (seven or more with more than 100 feet high), crystal clear emerald water, and great vertical and horizontal elements. Lots of flat rocks, logs, and some beach to camp out on. Further up, there are just loads of cliffs and falls to jump from. It really is paradise on earth.

Restaurant and Bathrooms:

There is a general store in Orville to stock up. There are no restrooms at the trailhead parking. In fact, there is no real trailhead.

Information and Contact:

There is no fee. For a map of Plumas National Forest, please contact the office or visit the website at www.fs.fed.us/r5/maps/. For more information, please contact the Plumas National Forest, Feather River Ranger District, 875 Mitchell Ave., Oroville, CA 95965, 530/534-6500, website: www.fs.fed.us/r5/plumas.

For a video of the Seven Falls please visit our website at:

http://swimmingholesofcalifornia.blogspot.com

Highlights

There are a number of great waterfalls in the area. If you have time, plan to visit Feather Falls.

SEVEN FALLS

Driving Directions:

From Hwy. 70 in Oroville, take the Oroville Dam Blvd. exit (Hwy. 162 east and drive 1.6 miles to Olive Hwy./Hwy. 162. Turn right on Forbes Town Rd. and drive six miles. Turn left on Lumpkin Rd. and drive 10.8 miles. Turn left at the sign and look for the sign for Feather Falls. Reset your odometer and continue on Lumpkin Rd., past the Feather Falls turnoff. At 1.2 miles past the Feather Falls turnoff, take the right fork onto FS Rd. 27. At 7.9 miles, stay straight at the junction; this puts you on Rd. 94. At 14.5 miles, reach a major fork and turn right. At 16.2 miles, bear left. At 19.0 miles, take the left fork off of the pavement and onto the dirt road. At 19.4 miles, take the left fork onto Rd. 22N62, Milsap Bar Rd. At 21.7 miles you will see a good size clearing to park on the road. The trail is easy to find and descends down quite steeply. There is the remains of an old refrigerator nearby that marks the route.

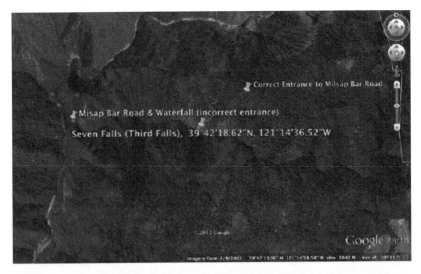

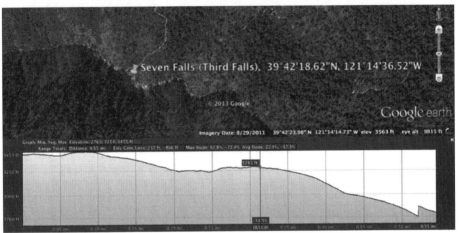

GOLD COUNTRY & YUBA RIVER

Tahoe National Forest off Hwy. 49
Access: Hike 1.5 miles one way (3.0 round trip)
Level: Moderate

Bathrooms nearby: No
Water Temperature: Cold
Clothing Optional: Yes, private pool
Dog/Kid friendly: No
Best Season: July through September

Here is the ideal couple's swimming hole. A great place to bring a picnic basket, blanket, your sweetheart, and spend the day. A 12-foot fall churns into the tub and pool below. Depending upon the time of year you visit will determine how much water is flowing from the falls. It's like regulating the faucet on the bathtub. Come in the spring and early summer for high flows, or later in the summer and early fall for a lower flow rate. The small canyon and falls gives you the feeling of enclosure or like being in a room. There are a number of beautiful trees and plant life is abundant. The tub is about 8 to 10 feet deep. There is a little five-foot ledge for jumping. If you wanted to try your luck you could probably jump right off the 15-foot mark at the lip of the falls.

There are numerous places to stop and swim along the way to Cherokee Creek. The trail and hike are fairly flat. The trail is located on the right embankment just before the wooden bridge that crosses the creek. There is also a trail that runs along the creek. That is the wrong trail. It will not take you to the falls.

There are a number of interesting stone walls that remain from the early mining camps that were built. Just after the stone wall is a large fir tree the evidently survived the logging days. The trail is fairly steep in some places and you may be forced to cross over a few downed trees in the trail.

This swimming hole has a good vertical and great horizontal element. There is plenty of space for sunbathing and relaxing. Further, the falls face south and stay heated by the sun even into the late Fall. This makes the water temperature moderate for most of the year. The parking area here is flat and quite large. Overall, a great expectation of privacy, and great swimming hole.

Restaurant and Bathrooms:

The closest bathrooms are at the Oregon Creek swimming area. The last gas station with food is 1 to 2 miles south of the Bridge over the Middle Yuba River.

Information and Contact:

There is no fee to enter this area.

For additional photos and a video, please visit our website at:

http://swimmingholesofcalifornia.blogspot.com

Highlights

There is a small place to camp about 0.5 miles from the parking lot. Shenanigan Flats is generally open all year round and allows travel trailers.

CHEROKEE CREEK

Driving Directions:

From Nevada City, drive north on SR 20 for 0.4 miles to SR 49. Drive north on 49 for 29.75 miles to the bridge over the North Yuba River. Park on the west side (cross over the bridge and turn left at end of the guardrail). Take the Canyon Creek Trail (which is a dirt road) for about 1.5 miles to a wooden foot bridge. The trail is up the right embankment and is very easy to miss. It's about 0.25 miles to the falls and swimming hole from that point.

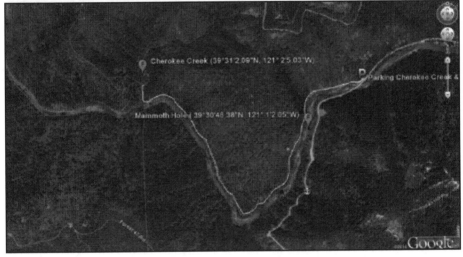

CHEROKEE CREEK

GOLDEN QUARTZ

Just outside of the Town of Washington on the South Fork of the Yuba River (Tahoe National Forest)
Access: No hike required.
Level: Easy

Bathrooms nearby: Yes in the parking lot of the picnic area
Water Temperature: Moderate/warm
Clothing Optional: No
Dog/Kid friendly: Yes
Best Season: July & August
Note: No real hike to this swimming hole

Golden Quartz is easy to reach and access, yet maintains a fairly high level of privacy all year round. It's remarkable given that it is located at the parking area of the Golden Quartz picnic area. It's never crowded, the water is beautifully clean, and there is a jumping rock and small rope swing. What else could you ask for?

Golden Quartz is situated on the South Yuba River near the town of Washington, just off of Hwy. 20. This little town in Nevada County is located on the banks of the South Fork of the Yuba River. It is located off Hwy. 20 between Nevada City and Interstate 80. Washington boasts a population on about 200, but that fluctuates seasonally and the town has a lot of tourist traffic in the summer.

Washington was founded in 1849, as were most of the cities in Nevada County; it was all about the Gold Rush! These particular miners were from Indiana, so the settlement was first named Indiana Camp, but renamed to Washington in 1850. The area produced a large amount of placer gold, after that hard rock and hydraulic mines were established and were also very productive. Many people of Chinese descent worked in the area at these times.

Now most of the miners are gone, yet the wonderful swimming holes remain for all to enjoy. The horizontal element is quite good given that there is a nice sandy beach here. It's a great place to bring a few lawn chairs, a cooler, and just sit back and enjoy the water, the river, and the great outdoors. The vertical element comprises a large jumping rock and a rope swing that is across the river on the other side.

Restaurant and Bathrooms:

The closest bathrooms are located in the parking area of the Golden Quartz picnic area.

Information and Contact:

There is a fee to enter this area.

Highlights

There are a number of other nice swimming holes at the bridge you must cross to get to Golden Quartz.

Driving Directions:

From the town of Washington take Maybert Rd. out of town until the end. The end is the Golden Quartz campground and picnic area. Near the end of the journey you will cross an old bridge. The road closest to the camping area gets quite rough and may require four-wheel drive. Keep driving until you hit the parking lot and camping area.

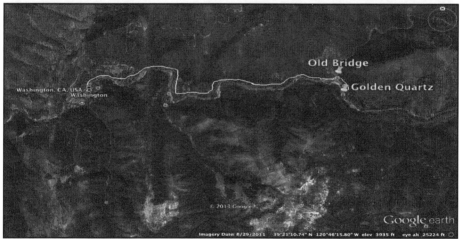

LOWER EMERALD POOLS

Tahoe National Forest, off of Hwy. 20 and Bowman Rd
Access: Hike 0.5 miles one way (1.0 miles round trip)
Elevation: Starts at 4515 feet; Loss of 0 feet
Level: Difficult

Bathrooms nearby: No
Water Temperature: Cold
Clothing Optional: No
Dog/Kid friendly: Not kid or dog friendly
Best Season: July, August, & September

The North portion of the Yuba River has some outstanding swimming holes. Lower Emerald Pools is one of them. A large 100-foot falls feeds into a deep gorge. In some places the cliff walls go up as high as 300 to 400 feet This is a cliff jumper's paradise. However, extreme care and caution should be exercised here. The underwater currents near the falls can be quite strong. Further, the water can be very cold until even the late summer. Given the strong currents of the river, combined with the hot canyon and deep gorge make for a fairly harsh environment. At the entrance of the trail a number of memorials have been established for those people killed here. Many of these accidents were due to jumping from the high cliffs or were alcohol related. Further, it's been reported that a number of people jumping near the falls have been caught by undercurrents that pushed them under rocks deep in the water after they jumped. So extreme caution should be exercised when attempting any jumps.

Lower Emerald pools is definitely one of the best swimming holes in the state of California and boasts both strong vertical and horizontal elements. Across the river is a small beach for setting up camp, some chairs, and relaxing.

The trail and hike down to the river is not far, but the going is often slow due to the steep nature of the rocks. Further, in certain places the trail becomes lost. However, Lower Emerald Pools is one of those places that you should at least plan to visit once during a summer.

The trail to Lower Emerald pools is just past the bridge on Bowman Rd. It's actually up around the corner across from the second parking area. You will know you are on the right trail if you climb a small knoll and hike a short distance to see the memorial sites. Continue on the trail and stay to the right as you face the river. The path is well worn, but can get lost in places. Keep following the trail until you reach the gorge area. There is some poison oak so be careful!

Restaurant and Bathrooms:

The closest bathrooms are on Bowman Rd.

Information and Contact:

There is no fee here.

For additional photos, please visit our website at:

http://swimmingholesofcalifornia.blogspot.com

Highlights

If you don't want to climb down the steep cliffs, hike to Upper Emerald Pools. It's much more kid- and dog-friendly.

LOWER EMERALD POOLS

Driving Directions:

From Rt. 80 North, take the Rt. 20 exit. Follow Rt. 20 to Bowman Rd. Take Bowman Rd. until you reach the first bridge over the Yuba River. There is parking on the right side of the road. Use the first parking lot for Upper Emerald Pools and the second parking lot 0.1 miles further up on the right for Lower Emerald Pools. The trailhead for Upper Emerald Pools is in the far back left side as you face north (looking up river). The trail is on the left side of the river or the west side. For Lower Emerald Pools cross the road from the second parking area, climb the small hill and travel in a southwest direction until you reach the trailhead.

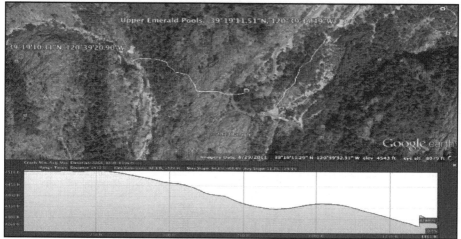

⭐8 UPPER EMERALD POOLS

Tahoe National Forest, off of Hwy. 20 and Bowman Rd
Access: Hike 05 miles one way (10 miles round trip)
Elevation: Starts at 4515 feet; Loss of 0 FT
Level: Easy

Bathrooms nearby: No
Water Temperature: Cold
Clothing Optional: No
Dog/Kid friendly: Yes
Best Season: July & August

Not wanting to hoof it all the way down the cliff to the gorge of Lower Emerald Pools? Try the short hike to Upper Emerald Pools. It's actually very easy to reach and receives a lot less traffic than Lower Emerald Pools.

A large oval pool is surrounded by a rocky beach and border. The swimming hole has both a good vertical and horizontal element. There are plenty of rocks to jump from and lots of rocks for relaxing. The surrounding rocks have an unusually beautiful texture and color. The swimming hole is as deep as 20 feet in some places. There is also a rope swing on the near side of the swimming hole. This is a great swimming hole that can accommodate all age groups. It's both a great swimming hole and a good family destination.

The privacy expectation is not bad. Some days you may have this place all to yourself. It's either not known by others or not visited frequently since it doesn't seem to garner the same crowds as Lower Emerald Pools.

Restaurant and Bathrooms:

The closest bathrooms are on Bowman Rd.

Information and Contact:

There is no fee here.

For additional photos, please visit our website at:

http://swimmingholesofcalifornia.blogspot.com

Highlights

If you want some higher cliffs or a challenging hike, hike to Lower Emerald Pools.

UPPER EMERALD POOLS

Driving Directions:

From Rt. 80 North, take the Rt. 20 exit. Follow Rt. 20 to Bowman Rd. Take Bowman Rd. until you reach the first bridge over the Yuba River. There is parking on the right side of the road. Use the first parking lot for Upper Emerald Pools and the second parking lot 0.1 miles further up on the right for Lower Emerald Pools. The trailhead for Upper Emerald Pools is in the far back left side as you face north (looking up river). The trail is on the left side of the river or the west side. For Lower Emerald Pools cross the road from the second parking area, climb the small hill and travel in a South West direction until you reach the trailhead.

UPPER EMERALD POOLS

MAMMOTH HOLE

Tahoe National Forest off Hwy. 49
Access: Hike 0.05 miles (1.0 mile round trip)
Level: Easy
Bathrooms nearby: No

Water Temperature: Moderate
Clothing Optional: No
Dog/Kid friendly: Yes
Best Season: July through September

If you haven't been to the Chilean resort of San Alfonso Del Mar, then you have not enjoyed the largest swimming pool in the world. It's roughly 1 kilometer in length and displaces approximately 6000 swimming pools.

Mammoth hole may roughly be one of the largest swimming holes. It's a huge patch of water measuring around 100 feet across. It's easy to find and provides plenty of room for the entire family. At the far upstream portion of the hole there is a large rock impound that can be used for jumping or diving.

There is a small private beach on the opposite side of the river. It would appear the only way to get there is to swim across the river.

This is the ideal swimming hole to pack a cooler, bring some floatation devices, and plan for a lazy and relaxing time. No real rapids or strong falls to worry about. This makes it an ideal swimming hole for small children.

The water in the spring and fall is a beautiful aquamarine. Just like aquamarine stones, the color of this swimming hole can vary from almost white pale blue to a slightly darker green or sky blue. In summary, a good swimming hole, but nothing particularly exciting about the vertical or horizontal elements.

Restaurant and Bathrooms:

The closest bathrooms are at the Oregon Creek swimming area.

The last gas station with food is 1 to 2 miles south of the bridge over the Middle Yuba River.

Information and Contact:

There is no fee to enter this area.

For additional photos and a video, please visit our website at:

http://swimmingholesofcalifornia.blogspot.com

Highlights

Bring a picnic basket, some sandwiches and refreshments and enjoy the river. Continue on the same trail past Shenanigan Flats to Cherokee Creek swimming hole.

MAMMOTH HOLE

Driving Directions:

From Nevada City, drive north on SR 20 for 0.4 miles to SR 49. Drive north on SR 49 for 29.75 miles to the bridge over the North Yuba River. Park on the west side (cross over the bridge and turn left at end of guardrail). Take the Canyon Creek Trail (which is a dirt road) for about 0.5 miles to a dirt trail on the left. Follow it down until the river.

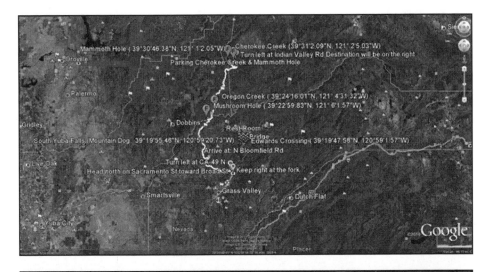

★ 6 MOUNTAIN DOG/SPRING CREEK

Edwards Crossing, Tahoe National Forest
South Yuba River State Park, off Hwy.
49 near Nevada City
Access: Hike 0.6 miles one way (1.2 miles round trip)
Elevation: Starts at 2,600 ft, total gain 200 ft
Level: Easy

Bathrooms nearby: Yes
Water Temperature: Moderate
Clothing Optional: Yes
Dog/Kid friendly: Yes
Best Season: July, August, & September

Here is a swimming hole for the bad planner. It's very easy to reach and the hike to the swimming hole is fairly easy and short. So if you wake up on a weekend a little bit later than you would have expected and decide it's too hot not to go swimming, than this is the place for you. The area under the bridge and just a little further down get most of the crowds. If you want to be more discriminating you can hike down the trail a little ways to the falls and the adult pools. The waterfall is formed by the intersection of Spring Creek and the South Yuba River. The falls are nice all year round. Particularly, in the spring time they can really flow at a hard rate. Still further down from the falls is a beach and a small pool. The pool is about 10 feet deep and about 60 feet in diameter. From time to time some adults have used the lower pools as clothing optional. In addition, early in the spring a number of kayakers like to run this section of the river.

MOUNTAIN DOG/SPRING CREEK

In order to reach the falls you need to cross Spring Creek. The falls is actually hidden from view until you are down on the sandy beach.

The 20-foot free-falling falls acts as a free-falling shower. Most swimmers approach the falls and take a quick shower under the falls. Imagine the coldest shower you've ever taken. Even on the hottest summer day that is what you will experience. However, it sure is refreshing.

Just alongside the waterfall is a small beach and a 40-foot strip of open water for swimming, bathing, and cooling off. One thing to consider is the fact that many people choose to wear their birthday suit instead of a swim suit.

The trail along the river and to the falls is not steep. It's, therefore, practical to take dogs and small children to any of the swimming holes. You might want to have someone scout ahead to avoid the embarrassment of the anatomy lesson for junior.

Restaurant and Bathrooms:

The closest bathrooms are at Edwards Crossing. The best restaurants are up the road in Grass Valley and Nevada City.

Information and Contact:

There is no fee to enter this area and park. For more information and a map/brochure, contact South Yuba River State Park, Bridgeport Visitor Center and Ranger Station, 17660 Pleasant Valley Rd, Penn Valley, CA 95946, 530/432-2546, website: www.parks.ca.gov.

For additional photos and a video, please visit our website at:

http://swimmingholesofcalifornia.blogspot.com

Highlights

This can be a popular place. There are a number of places to swim. The water temperature under the bridge tends to warm faster during the year.

MOUNTAIN DOG/SPRING CREEK

MOUNTAIN DOG/SPRING CREEK

Driving Directions:

EDWARDS CROSSING: Apparently a very popular (i.e., crowded) spot on the South Yuba, but quieter places are nearby. To get here from Nevada City, at the split of Rt. 20 and Rt. 49 in Nevada City turn left (sharp left) (Nevada City Carriage Company is on the right). Drive for about 1/4 of a mile or less. North Bloomfield Rd. is the second road on the right after Coyote Rd. (there is a fire station at the corner). Take North Bloomfield Rd. for about 1 mile until the "T" in the road and bear right. Follow North Bloomfield Rd. for about 8 miles until the South Yuba Recreation area and Edwards Crossing. The last mile of road to Edwards Crossing is very narrow and steep, so take it slow. The road is paved all the way until Edwards Crossing. It's much better to approach Edwards Crossing from the south side of the bridge. The road on the north side is not paved. Also, the parking is on the south side of the bridge and that is where the bathrooms are located.

This is a very popular place, so get there early since the parking can fill up quickly.

SOUTH YUBA FALLS: Where Spring Creek comes into the South Yuba there is a small falls and nice swimming hole — bathing suits optional. Park at Edwards Crossing (above), but avoid the crowds by hiking downstream on a trail along the north side of the river about a mile to the side creek and falls. The trail to "Spring Creek" is located on the north side of the bridge. It's easy to find and locate. The hike is about 1 mile to the creek and swimming holes. Here, and a bit further downstream, are the swimming places.

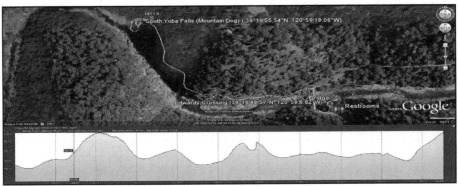

NORTH CANYON

North of Edwards Crossing (Malakoff Diggins State Park)
Access: Humbug Trail (9.0 or 10.0 miles round trip) or South Yuba Campground (5-6 miles round trip)
Level: Difficult

Bathrooms nearby: Yes
Water Temperature: Cold
Clothing Optional: Yes
Dog/Kid friendly: Yes
Best Season: July & August, too early in the year the water levels can be dangerous, too late in the year the water can be stagnant

Here is a swimming hole for hikers and mountain bikers. It's not easy to reach and requires a good hike or ride. There are two ways to reach the swimming hole. One route is via the Humbug Trail and the other originates from the South Yuba Campground.

North Canyon is a beautiful canyon with a bunch of swimming places in the South Yuba River upstream of Edwards Crossing. It's really a series of swimming holes formed along a winding constriction in the river. It's located at a bend in the river. In this canyon, the bend is quite dramatic and makes nearly a 150-degree turn. There is a broad rock ledge next to the river and an old miner's camp. There are plenty of places to jump or dive into the water. The water is about 15 feet deep in most places. The rocks and banks are easy to climb. The expectation of privacy is almost guaranteed.

FIRST WAY: first way is the easier, quite level, and about 5 to 6 miles round trip. To get there, from Edwards Crossing continue on North Bloomfield Rd. about 1 mile to signs for the South Yuba Campground. From the campground, hike the South Yuba Trail south to the river, then east along the river to North Canyon. The swimming holes are in North Canyon.

The hike to North Canyon via the South Yuba trail (South Yuba Campground) is much easier than the Humbug trail hike. Although this is still a very hot Canyon and people need to be advised to bring enough water (at least two bottles each). From the trailhead it's about 2 miles to Overlook Point and then another 1 mile to the North Canyon spur trail (this is the trail that heads down to the river with the switchbacks). There is a marker at the spur trail. The spur trail does not look like a trail since it's slightly overgrown. It's easy to miss and hikers need to note that it's right across from the marker sign in North Canyon. As you proceed down the trail it gets better. The trail down to the canyon has a number of switch- backs. It's about 0.4 miles. So the hike distance is about 6 to 7 miles round trip for this hike.

You can pick up the South Yuba Trail at the end of the upper parking area at the South Yuba campground. We recommend taking the North Bloomfield Rd. to Edwards Crossing, crossing the bridge and driving up the dirt road about 3 miles until you reach the South Yuba Campground exit. It will be on the right and descends down a hill. The road is dirt, but in good condition and easily drivable by any car. You proceed down the hill and come to a fork. You proceed to the right. The lower road goes to the campground. The upper road goes to the parking area. The parking area is obvious. You can park in this top lot. Note that there are bathrooms here. The trail to the South Yuba trail is actually not labeled and is at the back of this parking lot. You just follow this unmarked trail down and it will go for about 0.5 miles until you reach a sign indicating the South Yuba Trail. You will know you are on the right trail since it parallels the road to the campground which you will see from the trail. Note at this sign the South Yuba is to the left and goes up the slight incline.

At Overlook Point there are picnic tables, but no real view. The best view of the Canyon is about 0.2 miles from the North Canyon spur trail. You can see the entire canyon. We encountered a number of mountain bikers on this trail. The trail is fairly level with some slight inclines. We would rate it of moderate difficulty. However, it's a long way to the Canyon floor. We recommend this for the hike first and the swimming hole second. If you are going to use the swimming hole you need to leave early. Otherwise, you will find yourself reaching the hole and then having to hike back almost immediately to avoid hiking in the dark. The river flow is strong in May and nearly non-existent in September, so people need to plan accordingly. The canyon is also quite hot even in May.

SECOND WAY: The second way is more strenuous and begins in Malakoff Diggins State Park. To get there, from Edwards Crossing continue on North Bloomfield Rd. to Malakoff Diggins State Park (has camping). In the State Park, take the Humbug Trail (2.4 miles one way) then the South Yuba Trail (1.5 miles one way) down to the river and the swimming holes. The hike down the Humbug Trail is about 2.4 miles (there is a picnic table at the end of the trail to rest). The Humbug Trail is fairly steep so people should leave early since the hike is long and you don't want to be hiking up this trail in the dark due to the ledges. You must then pick up the South Yuba Trail and hike around another 1.5 miles to reach a series of switchbacks. This is a long hike. Then, after you hike the South Yuba trail you must take a series of switchbacks down to the river. This will deliver you to the hole. Note that this is really a 9 to 10 mile hike to the swimming hole and back. People really need to bring plenty of water on this hike. Visiting too early in the year the waters can be strong. In September, most of the water will have left the canyon so it's not as wonderful.

Restaurant and Bathrooms:

The closest bathrooms are at the South Yuba Campground. Restaurants are located in Nevada City or Grass Valley.

Information and Contact:

There is no fee here.

For additional photos, please visit our website at:

http://swimmingholesofcalifornia.blogspot.com

Highlights

If you get here too late, try the South Yuba Falls at Edwards Crossing.

NORTH CANYON

NORTH CANYON

Driving Directions:

See Description

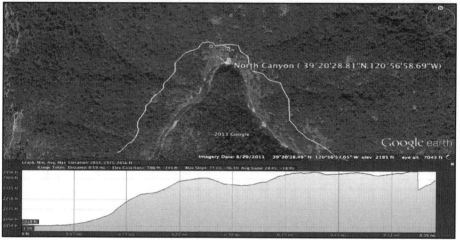

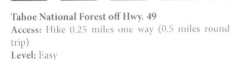

Tahoe National Forest off Hwy. 49
Access: Hike 0.25 miles one way (0.5 miles round trip)
Level: Easy

Bathrooms nearby: Yes
Water Temperature: Moderate
Clothing Optional: Yes
Dog/Kid friendly: No
Best Season: July & August

This Sierra Classic is nearly the perfect swimming hole. It's hidden yet accessible and is deep and not too narrow. It has both good vertical and horizontal elements. Plenty of space for laying out and sunbathing. This is a popular place for nudists and ladies that like to go topless. There is a posted sign warning that it's a clothing-optional swimming hole.

There are two sets of magnificent falls. The falls on the left step down in a stair-like fashion, while the falls on the right concatenate like a braided rope. They both meet together and spill into the 6- to 8-foot deep pool.

Diving should be avoided at Oregon Creek. There have been a number of injuries from swimmers diving into the water and hitting submerged rocks.

The falls are particularly fascinating because you can duck under them and totally submerge yourself without being seen. The space is about big enough to hold three people. Further up, there is a large pothole in the top step of the falls that feeds directly down into the rock and surfaces on the other side of the falls. Kids enjoy swimming through the channel to the other side.

Kids also like to use the rock as a small slide. Further, below there are a few Jacuzzis cut into the granite.

This swimming hole does not receive runoff from snow melt. For this reason, it maintains a fairly moderate temperature all year round. For those of you that don't like the cold Sierra water, this is your swimming hole!

Restaurant and Bathrooms:

The closest bathrooms are at Oregon Creek Camping area and beach about 0.5 miles away (right after you cross the bridge over the Middle Fork of the Yuba River). The closest gas station and Restaurants are about 2 miles away (south of the bridge).

Information and Contact:

There is no fee here.

For additional photos and a video, please visit our website at:

http://swimmingholesofcalifornia.blogspot.com

Highlights

You can take the kids to the swimming area just under the bridge over the Middle Fork of the Yuba River. No anatomy show there.

OREGON CREEK

Driving Directions:

To get there, set your odometer at the Middle Yuba Bridge and go a little under 1.0 miles north on Rt. 49 from the bridge over the Middle Yuba and park at a small turn off on the right side of the road (look closely, this turn off is not easy to find. Right before the turn off there is a rusted guardrail with a white road marker that says YUB 49. That is the first marker you will see while driving. Next to this marker and closer to the parking place is a second white marker that has the number 101 on it. If you still can't find it and are in doubt, the road is marked here with the number 213'). There is a big dirt hump at the parking area you go over to get to the trail. Walk a short way (.25 miles) or less down a well-maintained trail to Oregon Creek and the swimming hole.

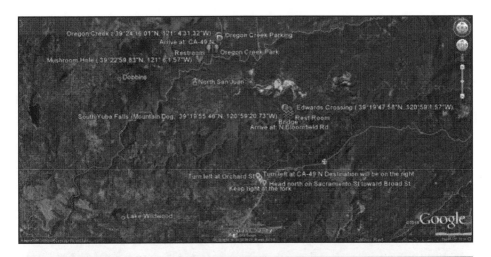

OREGON CREEK

SOUTH YUBA RIVER

Edwards Crossing, Tahoe National Forest South Yuba River State Park, off Hwy. 49 near Nevada City
Access: Hike varies based on the swimming hole you visit. The Bridge requires no hike. Cathedral is about 1.0 mile. Hoyt's Crossing is about 1.2 miles (One-way)
Level: Easy

Bathrooms nearby: Yes
Water Temperature: Moderate/warm
Clothing Optional: In some areas like Hoyt's Crossing.
Dog/Kid friendly: Yes
Best Season: Good to visit all year round

The Yuba River has some of the best swimming holes in the state of California. Further, if you don't like the swimming hole you are at just move up or down stream to find another better one. The large granite slabs help to warm the water.

You should arrive early if you plan to swim at the South Yuba area since the parking lot can fill up quickly. Just under the old Yuba bridge is the first swimming hole. This area is popular with families, teenagers, and small children that like a simple and hassle free environment to swim in. There are both strong vertical and horizontal elements. For instance, there are plenty of large rocks to layout and relax. There are also a few rocks for jumping into the water.

If you cross the old bridge, there is a trail on the northeast side of the bridge that leads up the hill along the side of the river. You can take this trail for about 1.0 miles to reach a second swimming hole called "Cathedral."

Large granite slaps jet 75 feet or more skyward right out of the river forming an enclosure similar to a large "Cathedral." The swimming hole is fairly long and is at least 20 feet deep. There are both strong vertical and horizontal elements.

Further up the river from "Cathedral" is legendary Hoyt's Crossing. This is a well-known swimming hole for those individuals that prefer to swim without a bathing suit. There is a large swimming hole greater than 50 yards in diameter and surrounded by a sandy beach. Just further up the river from here (less than 200 yards) is a granite playground that comprises large granite slabs for sunbathing and some water slides for sliding.

If you continue still further up the river you can reach Edwards Crossing.

Restaurant and Bathrooms:

The closest bathrooms are near the Old Bridge parking lot. The best restaurants are up the road in Grass Valley and Nevada City.

Information and Contact:

There is no fee to enter this area and park. For more information and a map/brochure, contact South Yuba River State Park, Bridgeport Visitor Center and Ranger Station, 17660 Pleasant Valley Rd, Penn Valley, CA 95946, 530/432-2546, website: www.parks.ca.gov.

For additional photos and a video, please visit our website at:

http://swimmingholesofcalifornia.blogspot.com

Highlights

This can be a popular place. There are a number of places to swim. The water temperature under the bridge tends to be warmer earlier in the year.

SOUTH YUBA RIVER

Driving Directions:

To get here from Nevada City, at the split of Rt. 20 and Rt. 49 in Nevada City turn left (sharp left) (Nevada City Carriage Company is on the right). Drive until you reach the first bridge over the Yuba River. Exit at the road on the south side of the bridge and park.

SANTA CRUZ & BOLINAS

Point Reyes National Seashore
Access: Hike 2.7 miles one way (5.4 miles round trip)
Elevation: Starts at 1000 feet; total loss of 500 feet
Level: Moderate to easy

Bathrooms nearby: Yes, at the trailhead
Water Temperature: Moderate
Clothing Optional: Yes
Dog/Kid friendly: Kid friendly/Dogs not allowed
Best Season: Good to visit all year round

Are you looking for a good swimming hole around San Francisco, but don't want to swim in the ocean? Bass Lake is the best place around. It has fresh water, a great vertical element for dropping down a towel, and a rope swing!

So what else could you want? How about a nice leisurely hike through some beautiful eucalyptus trees followed by a magnificent view of the Pacific Ocean!

Depending upon the time of year and the day you decide to visit Bass Lake will determine if you will be swimming here alone. Some weekends during the summer can get moderately busy. Most people like to pack a cooler, some towels, and sunbathe. Others like to swim and use the rope swing! The rope swing on Bass Lake is one of the best in the area. It's

BASS LAKE

located back further from the area that you access the lake. The trail to get there has lots of poison oak, so why not just swim over!

If you are really adventurous you can continue 1 to 2 miles past Bass Lake to beautiful Alamere Falls. It's one of the most magnificent falls in Northern, California. It free falls about 40 feet onto a beautiful sandy beach on the Pacific Ocean.

It's a scenic 2.7-mile coastal hike up from the parking lot, and the water's warm (warmer than the Pacific, at least) and clean. The trail has some shade, but in places can be a little exposed. You might want to consider some sun screen.

Pack a lunch and bring some extra water. You should plan on staying the entire day.

So what are you waiting for?

Restaurant and Bathrooms:

The closest bathrooms are at the trailhead.

Information and Contact:

There is no fee here.

For additional photos, please visit our website at:

http://swimmingholesofcalifornia.blogspot.com

Highlights

You can take the kids to the swimming area or continue further to the beach and Alamere Falls. Try your luck on the mighty rope swing!

BASS LAKE

BASS LAKE

Driving Directions:

From Hwy 1 in Marin, take your first left after Stinson Beach toward Bolinas. Make two left turns to stay on Olema Bolinas Rd. From the town of Bolinas, turn right on Mesa Rd. and follow it 4.6 miles; the parking lot is past the Bird Observatory at the end of the road. Take the Coast Trail, and follow it 2.7 miles until you see Bass Lake on your left.

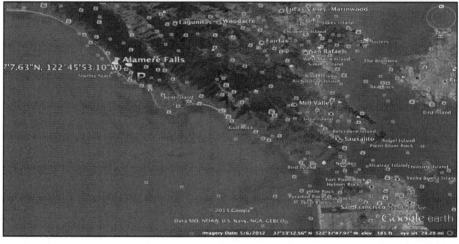

GARDEN OF EDEN

Henry Cowell State Park, San Lorenzo River near Felton in the Santa Cruz Mountains
Access: Hike 0.5 miles one way (1.0 mile round trip)
Level: Easy

Bathrooms nearby: No
Water Temperature: Moderate
Clothing Optional: Yes, but not encouraged by the state park
Dog/Kid friendly: Kid friendly/Dogs not allowed
Best Season: Good to visit all year round

Tired of taking those long trips to Yosemite National Park, but want to get away for a cool swim during a hot summer day? The Garden of Eden may be the place for you.

The Garden of Eden is located in Henry Cowell State Park. It's on the San Lorenzo River, near Felton in the Santa Cruz Mountains.

Just as the name describes it's a swimming hole paradise formed by a large rock impound positioned directly in the middle of a large bend in the San Lorenzo River. The swimming hole is lined by cobble, large beautiful fir and redwood trees, moss covered rocks, and two large sandy beaches.

A small falls feeds a 40-foot ellipse shaped pool formed at the front of the large rock impound. The pool is 8 to 10 feet deep in some areas. There is a nice jumping rock positioned on the central rock impound.

This is a popular place for families and kids in the summer, so the expectation of privacy should be considered low. It really depends upon the time of day and season. There are clothing-optional places just slightly above and below the main swimming area. On more than one occasion the author has bumped into Adam and Eve in their original clothing enjoying the river.

Although the state park does not encourage this behavior, there appear to be enough free spirits in Santa Cruz, so it does not matter. Be prepared to give junior an anatomy lesson if you decide to wander a little way off of the main beach area.

No real exciting vertical or horizontal elements but, hey, it beats driving four hours in the car to Yosemite National Park on a crowded weekend on a hot summer day.

Restaurant and Bathrooms:

The closest bathrooms and restaurants are in Felton.

Information and Contact:

There is no fee here.

For additional photos, please visit our website at:

http://swimmingholesofcalifornia.blogspot.com

Highlights

Grab a cooler, floatation device, and some refreshments and head to the Santa Cruz Mountains for the day. The Felton Train Station and park is just up the road. The kids will love it!

GARDEN OF EDEN

GARDEN OF EDEN

Driving Directions:

Directions begin at the main entrance to the Henry Cowell Redwood State Park which is about 6 miles north of Santa Cruz on Rt. 9, just south of Felton.

The first place is called the "Garden of Eden Beach" and is very beautiful. About 1.3 miles south of the park entrance (just south of the Toll House Resort) on Rt. 9 is a big turnout parking area on the east side (left) of Rt. 9. Park and walk past the gate on the right which has a small park rules sign. This is Ox Trail — take it steeply downhill and bear right to the railroad tracks. For Joyce's Beach, follow the dirt path across the railroad tracks. Some people call this Huck Finn's Hollow. There are some trails down to the river and small beaches near here.

Garden of Eden

To get to the Garden of Eden Beach, turn right and walk along the railroad tracks until you see a trail on the left and a sign. Descend down the trail for about 1/4 of a mile or less to the beach or swimming hole. Note that in and around the Garden of Eden some people have chosen to use this area as clothing optional. However, this is generally not encouraged by the park.

Big Rock Hole

Another place, at a deep, cool bend in the river, is called Big Rock Hole and is on the Rincon Trail. Drive south on Rt. 9 until you are about 3 miles south of the park entrance. There is a wide turnout on the east (left) side of Rt. 9 with a tree in the middle. The Rincon Fire Trail starts at the tree. Park and hike 1/2 mile downhill, wade across the river, then cross a sandy island to get to the swimming hole.

Frisbee Beach & The Dam

There are some other swimming places along the Rincon Trail where it turns left and follows the river. If you stay left all the way the trail goes for 1 to 2 miles to Frisbee beach. Note the other place to swim at is called the "Dam." There is a dam that forms a small swimming hole. This is just before Frisbee Beach.

Junction Park

Located in Boulder Creek, California, is a swimming hole just off of Middleton Ave. and Junction Ave. The park has a nice swimming hole, BBQ pits, picnic tables, and rope swing. Junction Park is a great place for kids, and a picnic. Bring a cooler, floatation device, and prepare to have fun. No hike required!

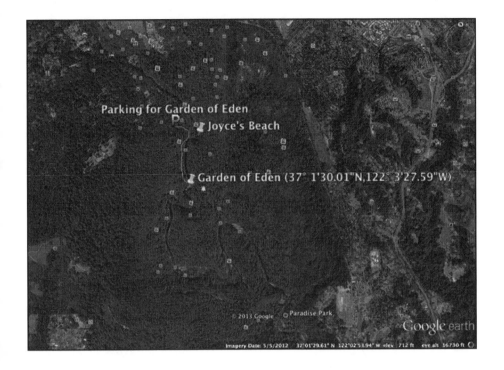

YOSEMITE &
CENTRAL SIERRA

CAMP NINE

Collierville, California (near Sonora, CA)
Access: Hike 0.5 miles one way (1.0 mile round trip)
Level: Easy
Bathrooms nearby: Yes

Water Temperature: Moderate
Clothing Optional: No
Dog/Kid friendly: Yes
Best Season: Good to visit all year round

Camp Nine is a swimming hole the locals like to keep secret. It's just too great a place to want to share. Most people know about Candy Rock and the legendary road to get there. As my friend said, "The road to Candy Rock is a once in a lifetime experience." The other happening place just outside of Sonora, California, is Camp Nine. The great thing about Camp Nine is the road is paved all the way to the parking area. In addition, there are bathrooms at the parking area. What else could you ask for? You got it, deep pools and great cliffs to jump from!

This swimming hole has much to offer. It has some of the best cliffs for jumping in Sonora, California. The walls are at least 50 feet in some places with a bottom that is nowhere in sight. The vertical element is also quite good with many places to drop a towel and relax. This is an ideal family swimming hole as well. There are many places along the trail where you can pull off and find your own private swimming spot.

This is a quite popular swimming hole. However, it never really gets too crowded. All around a great place that beats the crowds at Natural Bridges and Candy Rock.

Restaurant and Bathrooms:

There are bathrooms right at the parking lot. The closest gas station and restaurants are in Sonora, California.

Information and Contact:

There is no fee here.

For additional photos, please visit our website at:

http://swimmingholesofcalifornia.blogspot.com

Highlights

You can take the kids to the swimming area, bring a floatation device, or pack your own cooler.

CAMP NINE

Driving Directions:

From Sonora take CA-49 N (Parrots Ferry Rd). Cross the bridge over the Stanislaus River (New Melones Reservoir) and go past Natural Bridges. Continue up the hill and take a right onto Camp 9 Rd. Follow the Camp 9 Rd. all the way out to the power plant. It's paved all the way, but can get a little narrow in some spots. When you get to a second bridge that crosses the Stanislaus River stay left and continue toward the power plant. Camp 9 Rd. ends in a parking area that blocks access any further to the power plant. There is a bathroom there. Cross over the green metal bridge (walkway looks like you aren't supposed to use it, but it's available to the public) to the other side of the river and follow the trail straight for about 0.5 miles. There are a number of swimming holes. The photos were taken near the end of the trail, which is about 1.0 miles from the bridge.

CARLON FALLS

Stanislaus National Forest off Hwy. 120 near Yosemite
Access: Hike 3.0 miles round trip
Elevation: Starts at 4,500 feet; total gain 150 feet
Level: Easy

Bathrooms nearby: Yes, at parking area
Water Temperature: Cold year round
Clothing Optional: No
Dog/Kid friendly: Yes, flat walk to the falls
Best Season: Year-round

For many, Carlon Falls could be considered the perfect swimming hole. It's easy to reach, has bathrooms at the parking lot, the hike is not too long, and the falls are big and magnificent.

The hike starts on the north side of the bridge and river and tracks along the river for about 1 mile on fairly flat terrain. The trail then departs from the river and ascends for about 0.4 miles until you reach the falls. The trail is fairly easy and obvious to follow.

There are a number of spur trails that lead to the base of the falls. Getting to the base of the falls is fairly easy and this makes Carlon Falls an ideal place for families with children. The falls drop fairly steeply making the current not so strong and the oval swimming hole ideal for swimming.

Carlon Falls has a number of places to swim with both shallow and deep water. Further down from the falls there are a few rock impounds for jumping.

Carlon Falls has beautiful foliage that surrounds the falls and forest. The falls flow year round and are fed by a number of upstream tributaries. This makes the water fairly cold all year round.

Restaurant and Bathrooms:

Bathrooms are located at the parking area off of the road on the south side of the river. The closest supplies and super market are located in Groveland.

Information and Contact:

There is no fee. For a map of Stanislaus National Forest, please contact the office or visit the website at www.fs.fed.us/r5/maps/. Prior to making your trip you can also view the parking area and creek area using Google Earth. For more information, please contact the Stanislaus National Forest, Groveland Ranger District, 24545 Hwy. 120, Groveland, CA 95321, 209-962-785, website: www.fs.fed.us/r5/stanislaus.

For photographs of the falls, please visit our website at:

http://swimmingholesofcalifornia.blogspot.com

Highlights

You can take the kids to the swimming area, bring a floatation device, or pack your own cooler.

CARLON FALLS

Driving Directions:

From Groveland drive on Hwy. 120 for about 22 miles until the Evergreen turn-off on the left hand side (this is past the bridge of the Tuolumne River). Follow Evergreen Rd. down the hill for about 1 mile. The Carlon day-use area will be on the right. Cross the bridge and park on the right side (there is room for about five cars). There is additional parking and bathrooms on the side roads prior to the bridge. The trail begins on the north side of the river (behind the five-car parking area). The trail is worn and proceeds up river for about 1.4 miles (40 minutes).

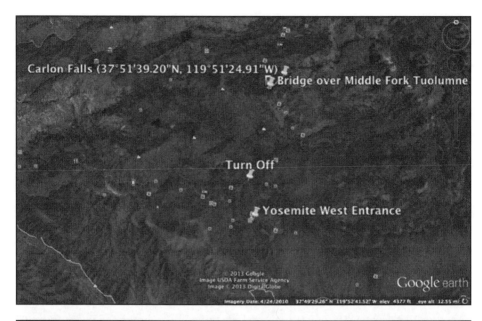

★6 CASCADE CREEK

Yosemite National Forest off Hwy. 120 near
Tamarack Campground
Access: Hike 2.4 miles one way (4.8 round trip)
Level: Moderate

Bathrooms nearby: Yes
Water Temperature: Cold
Clothing Optional: Upper tubs
Dog/Kid friendly: No
Best Season: August to early September

The hike to Cascade Creek is about 2.0 to 2.4 miles one way or 4-5 miles round trip. Save enough energy for the hike back since it's all uphill. You are also at fairly high elevation, so bring lots of extra water! This is a moderate level hike.

Just before you reach a prominent cluster of rocks (ideal for rock-climbing practice), your road begins a steady descent to Cascade Creek. At a road switchback just 240 yards before the bridge across this creek, you'll see a junction with a trail to the new Big Oak Flat Rd. Down at this lower, warmer, drier elevation you'll find Jeffrey and sugar pines intermingled with the firs. Along the first 200 yards below its bridge, Cascade Creek splashes down low cascades into small pools, and in late season these make nice "swimming holes." Before then the creek is likely to be too swift for safe frolicking, particularly since the water-polished rock can be quite slippery. Rooted in this creek are large-leaved umbrella plants, and growing just beside the water's edge are creek dogwoods, willows, western azaleas, and service berries. Huckleberry oaks crowd the dry rocks above the banks. Your day hike can be rounded out with a creek side picnic, under shady, spacious conifers, before you return to the campground. The picture's swimming hole is actually upstream from the bridge over Cascade Creek (about 0.25 miles). There is no real trail. The easiest way to the swimming hole is to start on the trail to the left of the creek. Then cross the creek and climb the hill. Then cross back over the creek at the base of the swimming hole. The water here is super cold even at the end of August! However, it serves as a very private and super couples swimming hole.

Restaurant and Bathrooms:

There are bathrooms at the Tamarack Campground. The last gas station with food and a bathroom is nearby at Crane Flat.

Information and Contact:

There is a fee since you must enter Yosemite National Park.

For additional photos, please visit our website at:

http://swimmingholesofcalifornia.blogspot.com

Highlights

Around mid-morning, Tamarack Flat Campground becomes temporarily abandoned, only to receive another flood of motorized campers in late afternoon. Take the time to enjoy the campground during the tranquil part of day. This is a very nice campground.

CASCADE CREEK

Driving Directions:

From Crane Flat drive northeast 3 3/4 miles up the Tioga Rd. to the Tamarack Flat Campground turnoff, immediately before the Gin Flat scenic turnout. Drive southeast down the old Big Oak Flat Rd. to the east end of Tamarack Flat Campground, 3 1/4 miles. The road is paved and slightly bumpy, but in good shape. The hiking trail is the actual road you are driving on. Access will be blocked at a turn-around point at the end of the campground. There are bathrooms at the campground.

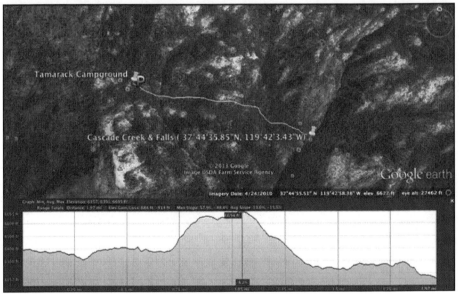

CLEO'S BATH

Stanislaus National Forest near Pine Crest Lake
Access: Hike 3.0 miles one way (6.0 miles round trip)
Level: Moderate

Bathrooms nearby: Yes, at Pine Crest Lake & Campground
Water Temperature: Cold
Clothing Optional: Upper tubs
Dog/Kid friendly: No
Best Season: July and August

No swimming hole book would be complete without Cleo's Bath. This is a great swimming hole located on the South Fork of the Stanislaus River that drains into Pine Crest Lake. This is an ideal place to spend the weekend. The campground at Pine Crest Lake can get quite busy in the summer, so you will need to plan ahead if you plan on renting one of the cabins on the lake. There is a nice trail that circles the lake. The beaches are quite nice and at the far end of the lake towards Cleo's Bath is a rock that people frequent and jump from. The hike to Cleo's Bath can be quite challenging. You will have to circle the lake, hike up a rocky incline, traverse a great forest, and then hike up a small cliff (3rd class scramble). The cliff climb is fairly safe, but can be challenging given the summer heat and the 6000-foot altitude.

Also, it should be noted that visiting Cleo's Bath too early in the year can be dangerous. The river in the spring rips through this valley and makes it completely unswimmable. Further, visiting too late in the year can also present a problem since the pools become stagnant and dark (September).

Restaurant and Bathrooms:

There are bathrooms at the Pine Crest Lake & Campground. There is food and water at the beach and campground. The nearest service station is about 2 miles up the road past the Stanislaus Ranger Station.

Information and Contact:

There is no fee for daily use. There is a fee if you rent a cabin and/or stay over-night.

For additional photos and video, please visit our website at:

http://swimmingholesofcalifornia.blogspot.com

Highlights

Around mid-morning, the campground starts to come alive. Pine Crest Lake has a beautiful beach and boating area. Why not plan ahead and make it a weekend stay.

CLEO'S BATH

Driving Directions:

From Sonora take State Rt. 108 east 28.7 miles to Pine Crest Rd. Bear right at the Stanislaus Ranger Station and continue 0.5 miles to the Pine Crest Lake & Campground. Follow the trail 1.5 miles around the right hand side of the lake. Follow the arrows and rock piles another 1.5 miles across a small forest to the base of the cliff. Ascend the cliff about 0.5 miles to reach Cleo's Bath.

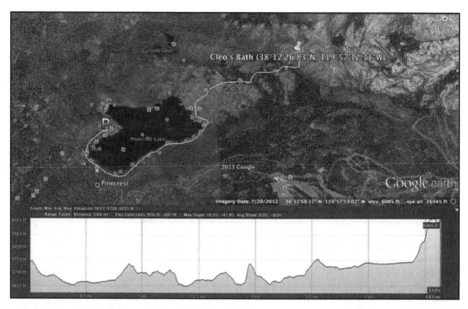

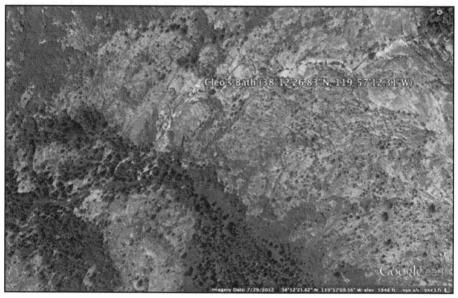

CONSUMNES RIVER

El Dorado National Forest, near Somerset
Access: Hike 0.25 miles one way (0.5 miles round trip)
Level: Easy

Bathrooms nearby: Yes
Water Temperature: Moderate
Clothing Optional: No
Dog/Kid friendly: Yes
Best Season: Good to visit all year round

You could spend 10 years living and traveling in California and not know a thing about this place. The locals like to keep this place a secret. Why not, it's the only swimming area which you can bring the kids and stop at a winery on the way home.

We describe two of the main swimming holes. There are a number of others in this area. You could probably find your own.

This is an ideal swimming hole because it doesn't require a long drive from any of the major California cities. There is also a natural preserve at the lower end of the Consumnes closer to Sacramento, California.

If you take the standard route or drive from Sacramento, California, you will pass by the Consumnes Preserve. This is really a good place for kayaking and bird watching. There is not much else going on there. You will then drive by the two large cooling towers of Rancho Seco Nuclear Power Plant. On March 20, 1978, a failure of power supply to the plant's non-nuclear instrumentation system led to steam generator dry-out. This was the third most serious nuclear power plant problem in the United States and led to a referendum to shut down the plant. Since then the associated land has been made a preserve and has been donated to the public.

Twin Bridges is the first swimming hole you can visit. It's very easy for kids, older people, and families to access. The river is not too deep and there is a small rope swing. It's located just under the bridge that crosses the Consumnes River. Many people bring their cooler, chairs, and floatation devices.

They call this twin bridges, because if you follow a small trail along the river, you will pass by a second bridge overpass. Just about 0.25 miles further down from there are a few good swimming holes. There is a good jumping rock here.

If you drive a little further along to Happy Valley Rd., you will come to two other swimming holes. The first is a small gorge area that usually has a limited expectation of privacy. Kids like this area to swim and snorkel to find beautiful stones that are scattered along the bottom of the river. This area usually has a low expectation of privacy. If you want additional privacy you can hike up the river a little way to a number of pot holes and swimming holes.

The Consumnes has carved a number of pot holes into the granite. If you continue even further up river you will pass under a bridge and then come to a large rock in the river that is difficult to pass and proceed any further. You will note the "No Trespassing" signs on the surrounding land. You should respect the landowner's requests.

Restaurant and Bathrooms:

The closest bathrooms are at the general store about 2 miles up the road. There are a number of wineries to eat at.

Information and Contact:

There is no fee here.

For additional photos, please visit our website at:

http://swimmingholesofcalifornia.blogspot.com

Highlights

You can take the kids to the swimming area just under the bridge over the Consumnes River. If you have extra time why not stop for some wine tasting?

CONSUMNES RIVER

CONSUMNES RIVER

CONSUMNES RIVER

Driving Directions:

From Sacramento, take Rt. 50 east about 40 miles, then take exit 44A for Missouri Flat Rd. Turn south (right) at Missouri Flat Rd. and go 1.7 miles then turn east (left) at Pleasant Valley Rd. Go 5.2 miles then turn south (right) at Bucks Bar Rd. Stay on Bucks Bar Rd. as it twists around until you come to Somerset. The directions below are from Somerset:

TWIN BRIDGES: This swimming hole is less than 20 yards from the road. It has a couple of small rope swings. A trail runs down the left side of the river to some additional holes and jumping spots (just past the second bridge). There are also some interesting rock formations here and a great jumping rock. To get there, in Somerset on Bucks Bar Rd., turn SOUTH (RIGHT) on Mt. Aukum Rd. (CR 116) and go about 1.5 miles until you cross the Consumnes River. Drive across the bridge and find the parking area on the east (left) side of the road behind the guardrail. (Note: Many people park on the next road (Paradise Rd). That is a no-no. You have to cross private property to get to the swimming hole, and there are signs posted telling you not to do this.

HAPPY VALLEY: Another set of swimming holes also in the Consumnes River that kids love. There are also a number of great rock formations and places for jumping. To get there, in Somerset on Bucks Bar Dr., continue straight onto Mt. Aukum Rd. (CR 116) NORTH. Continue on this road north until the four corners. Go straight through and the road will be the first one on your right as you start to descend down the road. It's easy to miss, but it's marked Happy Valley Rd. Follow this road for about 3 miles to reach the swimming holes. If you reach the bridge over the Consumnes River you have gone too far. The swimming holes are just downstream from the bridge.

DIANA FALLS

Stanislaus National Forest off Hwy. 120 near Yosemite
Access: Hike 1.0 miles round trip
Elevation: Starts at 3,100 feet; total loss 50 feet
Level: Easy

Bathrooms nearby: No
Water Temperature: Moderate
Clothing Optional: Lower tubs/Main pool, no
Dog/Kid friendly: No Steep walls to river
Best Season: April – October

Diana Falls is largely a swimming hole enjoyed by locals. It's fairly easy to reach and is set in the Stanislaus National Forest, not far from the towns of Groveland and Coulterville. It's about an hour drive from Yosemite National Park. Greeley Hill Rd. used to be the old entrance to Yosemite National Park. An added benefit's the fact that the road is paved all the way until the parking lot.

The trail to the falls is well worn and easy to find. It starts as a grass road and then narrows to a trail. It's located just beyond a metal gate and tracks along the river until it reaches the confluence with Bean Creek. At Bean Creek the trail turns sharply right and climbs for about 0.25 miles. There are a number of spur trails down to the river and swimming hole. The main trail circles around the canyon to the lip of the falls. The easiest route down is via a spur trail about 20 yards back from the vista point of the falls.

One hundred eighty degrees of rock forms this swimming hole. The falls are about 25 feet high and there are plenty of ledges and rocks for relaxing and sunbathing. Be careful getting down to the falls, there have been a number of injuries via the main trail. The granite walls are steep and when wet are very dangerous.

This is not an easy swimming hole to access and for this reason we don't recommend this swimming hole as being dog or kid friendly. It should also be noted that there are a number of easier to access and more private tubs further down from the falls.

The expectation of privacy is poor. Litter is generally not a problem, but from time to time graffiti shows up on some of the rock faces.

Although not a high theft area, please make sure to secure all valuables prior to leaving your car. From time to time rangers do patrol this area to prevent theft and vandalism.

Restaurant and Bathrooms:

There are a number of stores in Coulterville for supplies. The last gas station with food and a bathroom is at the top of the hill in Groveland.

Information and Contact:

There is no fee. For a map of Stanislaus National Forest, please contact the office or visit the website at www.fs.fed.us/r5/maps/. Prior to making your trip you can also view the parking area and creek area using Google Earth. For more information , please contact the Stanislaus National Forest, Groveland Ranger District, 24545 Hwy. 120, Groveland, CA 95321, 209-962-785, website: www.fs.fed.us/r5/stanislaus.

For a video of the falls please visit our website at:

http://swimmingholesofcalifornia.blogspot.com

DIANA FALLS

DIANA FALLS

DIANA FALLS

Driving Directions:

To get there from Coulterville, follow Main St. out of town to the east. Main St. becomes Greeley Hill Rd. Follow Greeley Hill Rd. up the hill and all the way until the Bridge over the North Fork of the Merced River. Greeley Hill Rd. forks at the top of the hill. Make sure to stay right at the fork. The trail is well marked and there is a gate near the parking area. The parking area will be on the left side of the road just before the bridge. If you cross the bridge and go too far, the road changes to dirt. The hike in is about 1 mile to the confluence of Bean Creek. The falls are about 200 yards further up the trail on Bean Creek and will be on your left. Also, there are a few tubs downstream from the falls. They tend to be clothing optional and hidden.

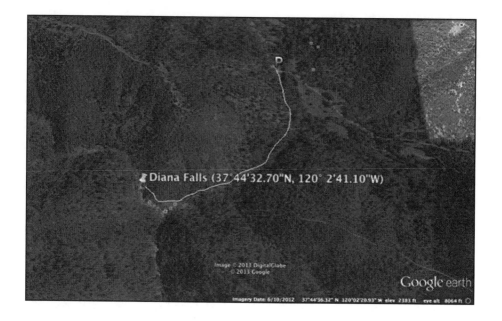

FISH CAMP FALLS

Sierra National Forest, off of Hwy. 41 near Fish Camp
Access: Hike 0.25 miles one way (0.5 miles round trip)
Elevation: Starts at 5400 feet; total gain of 250 feet
Level: Easy

Bathrooms nearby: Yes
Water Temperature: Moderate
Clothing Optional: No
Dog/Kid friendly: Yes
Best Season: Good to visit all year round

Fish Camp Falls is not one waterfall, but three. This swimming hole has a steady supply of water all year round. The three falls are all about 25 feet high. The most user friendly fall is the one furthest from the trailhead. Each of the falls free falls off of a similar granite ledge that runs about 300 yards in length.

There is plenty of parking just off of Big Sandy Rd. You will know when you are close to the trailhead because the road splits at a large tree in the middle of the road (there is a wooden fence there also). The trail begins at a metal gate. You pass through the metal gate and follow the trail past an old abandoned cabin. The trail tracks along a flume for about 0.5 miles until you reach the first falls. The other two falls are about 200 yards beyond the first falls. The trail ends at the top of the last falls. The vertical element is slightly better than the horizontal element. No real great places for jumping. Later in the year the granite can dry in places to make large granite slabs for sunbathing and relaxing. Occasionally, campers will set up camp in the area just beyond the metal gate and post signs indicating "no entry allowed." This is not common and is generally not encouraged by the park service. Just ignore the signs and try to avoid the camps by more closely tracking along the flume. It should not be an issue. In most cases, this will only happen on really busy weekends because some discourteous hikers have hiked directly through the camps. The falls, however, are on public land and can be enjoyed by all.

Restaurant and Bathrooms:

The closest restaurant and bathrooms are at the Tenaya Lodge.

Information and Contact:

There is no fee here. For a map of the Sierra National Forest, please visit the website at www.fs.fed.us/r5/maps/. You can also contact Sierra National Forest, Bass Lake Ranger District, 57003 Rd. 225, North Fork, CA 93643.

For additional photos, please visit our website at:

http://swimmingholesofcalifornia.blogspot.com

Highlights

You can mountain bike to the swimming hole and ride all the way up Big Sandy Rd. Also, just further up the road is the Skinny Dip swimming hole. Bring your fishing rod and reel. Big Creek is full of rainbow trout.

FISH CAMP FALLS

Driving Directions:

To get there from Oakhurst, drive north on Rt. 41 for 15 miles to the turn off on Big Sandy Rd. (a.k.a. Jackson Rd.) about 0.5 miles south of Fish Camp. Now set your odometer. Turn east (right) and drive 2.5 miles to a dirt pullout on the right. On the left is a metal gate. Go past the gate and follow the trail past an old abandoned cabin. The trail tracks along the flume for about 0.5 miles until you reach the first falls. The other two falls are about 200 yards beyond the first falls.

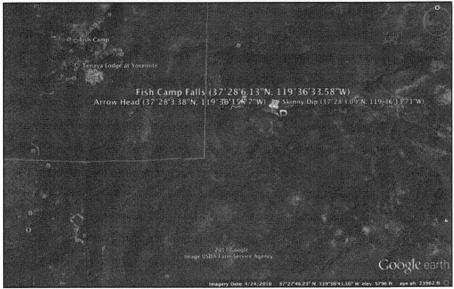

FISH CAMP FALLS

GLEN AULIN

Yosemite National Park, off Hwy. 120 near Tuolumne Meadows
Access: Hike 9.0 to 10.0 miles round trip
Elevation: Starts at 8600-9100 ft.
Level: Difficult

Bathrooms nearby: Yes, at trailhead
Water Temperature: Cold
Clothing Optional: No
Dog/Kid friendly: No
Best Season: June - August

This is the "Epic Swimming Hole Hike." There are so many swimming holes on this hike you will become a river Otter before it is over.

Parking is best at the Lembert Dome/Soda Springs parking area (this is the day use parking area). From there you hike out a number of miles (about 3.4 miles) until you reach the Tuolumne River. From there you will encounter a number of massive swimming holes and granite slabs. As you descend down the grand waterfall corridor you come upon more slab swimming holes and great places for enjoying the sun. Still further down, you can reach Tuolumne Falls, and then White Cascade/Glen Aulin Falls. The High Sierra Camp is located at the base of White Cascade/Glen Aulin Falls. For those that are even more adventurous you can continue down further to California Falls, Leconte Falls, and Waterwheel Falls. Waterwheel Falls is about 3.0 to 3.8 miles beyond the High Sierra Camp.

We do not recommend the trip all the way to Waterwheel Falls in one day. That's beyond the level of many hikers, never mind swimming hole enthusiasts. However, we mention it here because the nature of the hike and trail can provide something for everyone. For instance, if you really want to hike and see some additional waterfalls you can hike on while the others in your group stay at the other falls or even upper slabs and pools. Essentially, you will have to hike back up the same trail you came down and can then later join the other members in your group that decided not to go on. It makes for a great time for all.

Further, the beauty about this hike is that you can stop anywhere along the way and pick your own swimming hole to relax. We recommend that you leave early in the morning and hike all the way down to the High Sierra Camp. If you leave by 7 a.m., you will be there before it gets really hot. From there you can eat lunch, and then take your time hiking back up the trail (budget about four to five hours). We now describe each of the swimming holes you will encounter if you hike all the way out to the High Sierra Camp and then venture back up (swimming holes listed from bottom of the hike to the top of the hike).

Glen Aulin/White Cascade Falls:

Glen Aulin is almost 2000 feet higher than the other swimming holes we listed in this book. However, it was just so photogenic and beautiful that we couldn't resist listing it here. Further, although the camp is nearby and there are some man-made structures, we are sure you will agree that this is really wild and unique Sierra country, worthy of listing it in almost any swimming hole book.

The hole at the bottom is about 100 feet wide and nearly about the same distance wide. The falls drop about 40 to 50 feet down into a flat pool. Water depth was hard to gauge and will depend upon the time of year. Not much of a strong vertical element unless you want to head up to the top of the falls. The horizontal element boasts a nice sandy beach and access from right next to the High Sierra Camp. The water is cold all year round, and the color is that fabulous Yosemite emerald.

Tuolumne Falls:

The next falls on the way up is Tuolumne Falls. This is another 100-foot waterfall that steps down to a beautiful oval and elongated pool. Water depth is at least 15 to 20 feet at high flow times.

Lower Slabs:

Just above Tuolumne falls, but below the footbridge are a number of mundo rock slabs, falls, and pools. There are so many that you may want to just skip going down the steep grade to the bigger falls and stay here.

Upper Slabs:

Just after you encounter the river for the first time, the trail crosses a number of smooth granite slabs. There is a small five-foot gentle falls and water slide located here just next to a rounded granite dome. Water depth can vary from 6 to 10 feet depending upon the season. Although there is no vertical element here, the horizontal element and slabs are quite fabulous.

Restaurant and Bathrooms:

There is a bathroom at the Lembert Dome trailhead. Across the street is the Tuolumne Grill.

Information and Contact:

There is a fee to enter this area. A wilderness permit is required for overnight stays. You can obtain them online or at the wilderness kiosk at the trailhead. They are free and on a first come first serve basis. For more or additional information, contact Yosemite National Park, CA 95389, 209/372-0200, website: www.nps.gov/yose.

For a video of the falls, please visit our website at:

http://swimmingholesofcalifornia.blogspot.com

GLEN AULIN

GLEN AULIN

Driving Directions:

From Groveland, drive about 70 miles to Tuolumne Meadows (about 1.5 hours). The trailhead will be the first turnoff on your left after you reach Tuolumne Meadows. Alternatively, you can stay in Lee Vining if you plan ahead. From there the distance is about 20 miles (about 40 minutes), until you reach the trailhead. Park at the parking lot marked Dog Lake/Lembert Dome/Soda Springs. It will be on your left if you drive from Groveland and your right if you leave from Lee Vining. Start hiking at the gated dirt road just next to the Dome and horse stables. The gated dirt road has a sign that says "Soda Springs 0.5 miles."

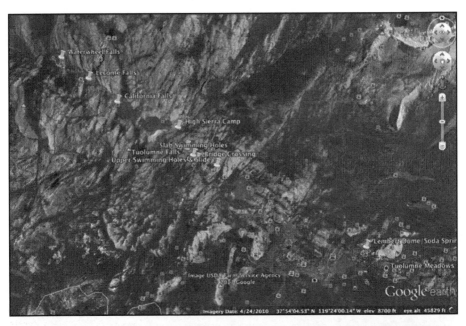

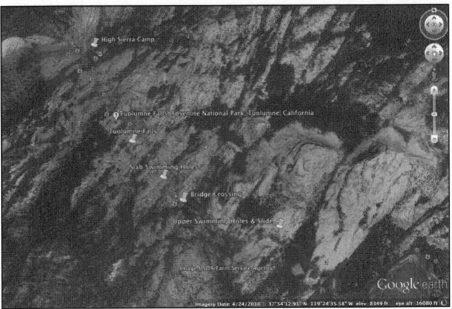

GOD'S BATH

Sonora, CA
Access: Hike 0.5 miles one way (1.0 mile round trip)
Elevation: Starts at 6000 feet; total loss of 100 feet
Level: Moderate

Bathrooms nearby: No
Water Temperature: Cold
Clothing Optional: No
Dog/Kid friendly: No
Best Season: July, August & September

Here is a swimming hole fit for the gods. God's Bath is considered by many to be the best swimming hole in Sonora, California. We would agree and add that we believe it may be one of the best in the state of California.

With great swimming holes, it's all about the rock formation and impounds. God's Bath is no exception. It comprises a low angle slab which occupies about 300 square feet. feet around a steep and narrow hole. The main pool is about 10 to 12 feet deep and remains that way through the entire summer. The rock impound forms an 8- to 10-foot rim around the main pool. The rim is at the perfect height for jumping. There is a small falls or chute to the back of the main rock impound that flows into the main tub. The main tub extends further downstream forming a contiguous series of figure eights. The eastern side of the swimming hole has a large area for sunbathing. The western side has a wall that goes up around 150 feet and provides a few jumping opportunities for daredevils. The highest probably being round 55 to 60 feet.

There is a large pot hole to the right of the main tub. It's around 10 feet to the water and connects to the main tub via an underwater channel. It's a favorite for locals to jump into and access the main tub.

At the front of the main tub is an underwater rock plateau that allows for ease of access and exit from the water. Up beyond the falls there is also space for sunbathing or enjoying the view.

God's Bath is one of those places everyone enjoys. It has both strong vertical and horizontal elements. It also is a fairly easy hike to get to. The most difficult part of the hike is getting down from the bridge to the river. The author has tried all kinds of routes. The easiest is the route that descends the canyon on the eastern side. You pick up the small trail just after the guardrail. There is a third class scramble down to the river. There is a rope provided to help with the climb down. For this reason, this is not really a good place for older people or young children. The hike down would just be too difficult.

There has been a lot of confusion regarding God's Bath and its location. The author has encountered more people lost going to this swimming hole than any other. Part of the reason is the lack of information regarding directions. The other reason is that some people have intentionally posted wrong directions to keep the place secret! So people pay attention here! The road to God's Bath is paved all the way to the bridge and beyond! If you are on a dirt road, you are going the wrong way!

There are a few things to remember about God's Bath. First, you will be at high elevation, so bring extra water! Second you will be in a hot canyon, so bring extra water! In addition, there are no bathrooms nearby or gas stations. So make sure to gas up prior to entering the road down into the canyon. Otherwise, it's going to be a white knuckle ride for 20 miles while your friends pray that you have enough gas to make it back.

Restaurant and Bathrooms:

The closest bathrooms and restaurants are in Sonora, California.

Information and Contact:

There is no charge to enter this area. Please note that if you have any questions or emergencies, the point of contact is the Mi-Wuk Ranger Station.

For additional photos and a video, please visit our website at:

http://swimmingholesofcalifornia.blogspot.com

Highlights

This is a great place for a picnic.

GOD'S BATH

GOD'S BATH

GOD'S BATH

GOD'S BATH

GOD'S BATH

Driving Directions:

From Sonora, take State Rt. 108, 2.4 miles to Tuolumne Rd. and turn right. Drive 9.5 miles to the town of Tuolumne. Take Buchanan Rd. out of town (also known as Cottonwood Rd.). The Forest Service roads are confusing. However, this would be FS N101. It's the only road paved over the Clavey River. You should follow this around 19 miles to the bridge over the Clavey River. There is a small parking area on the far side of the bridge that will be on your right. The bridge over the Clavey is fairly high. There is a sticker on the bridge that says "no bungee jumping." The descent to the river is on the eastern side of the river just behind the guardrail. The trail down is fairly steep and there is a rope to aid in the descent. Once you reach the bottom, proceed up the right-hand side of the river. If it's late enough in the season you will be able to hike directly up the river. In most cases though, you will reach a point where you need to climb on a small ledge at the right side of the river. The ledge can be a little tricky. There is a small rope to help you. Once you make it past this section of the river it's about 0.5 miles of hiking until the swimming hole. It's best to stay on the right-hand side all the way.

Note: When you first enter Cottonwood Rd., the canyon seems a little steep. This is actually the most difficult part of the road. It flattens out and is paved all the way to Cherry Lake. Don't forget to gas up!

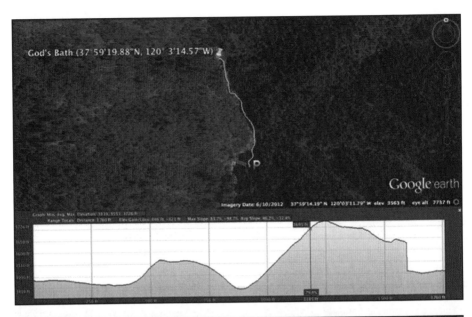

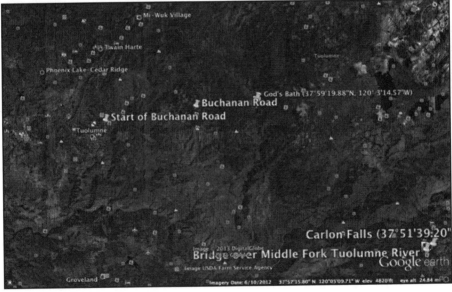

INDIAN FALLS

Mokelumne National Forest, off of Hwy. 88 near
Pioneer (east of Jackson & Volcano)
Access: Hike 0.25 miles one way (0.5 miles round
trip)
Elevation: Starts at 4500 feet; total gain of 100 feet
Level: Easy

Bathrooms nearby: Yes
Water Temperature: Moderate to cold
Clothing Optional: Maybe early spring
Dog/Kid friendly: No
Best Season: May–August

The Mokelumne Wilderness is a federally designated wilderness area located 70 miles east of Sacramento, California. It's within the boundaries of three national forests: Stanislaus, Eldorado, and Toiyabe. First protected under the Wilderness Act of 1964, the Mokelumne's (pronounced moo-ka-la-mi) borders were expanded under the California Wilderness Act of 1984. The wilderness takes its name from the Mokelumne River, which was named after a Mi-wok Indian village located on the riverbank in California's Central Valley.

Indian Falls is a beautiful swimming hole that you can sometimes have all to yourself. It's particularly designed for small groups and couples. A 5- to 8-foot waterfall empties into a beautifully carved 20 to 30 feet wide hole. The emerald water is constantly flowing and for this reason is clean almost all year round. The hole appears to be about 12 to 15 feet deep closest to the falls. A small underwater rock shelf provides for ease of access and exit from the water. There are both strong vertical and horizontal elements. The vertical element comprises a cliff next to the falls that is about 35 feet high. It provides a possible jumping opportunity for a limited few braves.

The horizontal element includes numerous places for sunbathing and rocks to recline and relax on to the side of and below the falls. The hole is bisected with what appears to be a possible killer water slide that empties into a larger pool below. In the spring small flowers can be seen growing on the cliff closest to the falls.

Please exercise extreme caution hiking to and from the swimming hole and accessing the water. The trail becomes fairly steep and the rocks can be slippery. You don't want to slip and find yourself bouncing down the rocks.

Restaurant and Bathrooms:

The closest bathrooms are at the general store or gas station located in Pioneer, California, or just off of Rt. 88 near the entrance to Tiger Creek Rd.

Information and Contact:

There is no fee here.

For additional photos, please visit our website at:

http://swimmingholesofcalifornia.blogspot.com

Highlights

There are other swimming holes nearby and around the river. If you continue to drive on Rt. 88 you can find some great views of the area and mountains at higher elevation. Further, up the road some way is Silver Lake and the Kirkwood ski area.

INDIAN FALLS

Driving Directions:

From Jackson, take Rt. 88 toward the Mace Meadow Country Club. Just prior to reaching the golf course take Tiger Creek Rd. for about 2.5 miles until you reach a large bend in the road. Park and look for a small trail on the northwest side of the bend in the road. Indian Falls is actually on Mill Creek that empties into the Tiger Creek Reservoir.

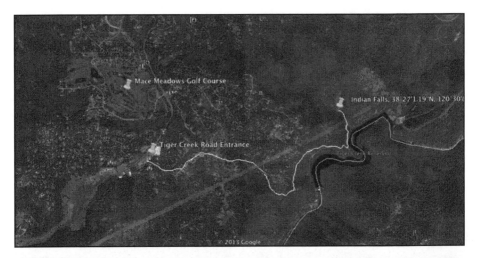

THE LEDGE

Yosemite National Forest off Hwy. 49
Access: Hike 0.5 miles one way (1.0 miles round trip)
Level: Moderate

Bathrooms nearby: Yes
Water Temperature: Cold
Clothing Optional: Yes, upper tub
Dog/Kid friendly: No
Best Season: July & August

This swimming hole comprises a large ledge spanning around 200 feet with varying depth between 2 and 8 feet, depending upon the time of year.

The vertical element for jumping is best near the falls.

There are a number of clothing optional tubs further up the cliff. They are not easy to reach and require you to scale up the cliff and dirt on the far right side of the hole. There is a small trail that leads to the top. You must then tip toe across a small ledge and part of the cliff to make it to the upper tubs. In other books this tub has been named "Honeymooners." I've spoken with a number of couples that have enjoyed the use of this upper tub. Many regard it as clothing optional because it's not easy to reach, and you can see people below you coming up the creek, but they can't see you.

Getting to The Ledge and Honeymooners is not an easy thing. They both require climbing up a third-class scramble. The ledge is much easier and is a great place for swimming with lots of friends.

Restaurant and Bathrooms:

The closest bathrooms are at the base of the Chilnualna Trail. There is a gas station and a restaurant at the Wawona Inn which is less than a mile away.

Information and Contact:

There is a fee to enter Yosemite Park.

For additional photos, please visit our website at:

http://swimmingholesofcalifornia.blogspot.com

Highlights

Plan ahead and stay overnight at the Wawona. There are places to BBQ and play golf nearby.

THE LEDGE

263

THE LEDGE

Driving Directions

From Oakhurst drive north on SR 41 and enter Yosemite Park. There is an entrance fee, unless you opt to get the annual pass (which is a good idea if you go to swimming holes regularly). Turn left at the entrance and head toward the Wawona. Take the first right onto Chilnualna Rd. just past the Wawona. It's about 1.5 miles on this road. It's a little tricky because it winds through a number of cabins. The trailhead parking is not so clear. It's right next to the bathrooms. If you get to a small bridge that crosses the creek, you have gone too far.

The trail has a small metal sign marking the path just to the left of the creek. There are two hiking options. The first is to follow the trail along the creek to the right. The other is to stay left of the trail and pick up the trail as it circles back to the left from the creek. It might be best to first take the trail along the creek to learn the trail and where you can pick it up.

The trail along the creek might not be suitable for small children since it becomes quite steep in places. Just along the lower falls there are a series of granite steps up the steep cliff.

The trail then comes to an end and with a switchback to the left. Instead of turning left continue straight up the steep embankment until you come to an area were the creek intersects the trail. There is a small falls here. You will then have to climb up a portion of the wall on the left side or try to cross the creek. Once at the top of this small ledge you will have to cross over a portion of the creek. There is a small island area with a tree and some rocks. From here you want to proceed up the cliff on the right side of the small falls. You will first have to wedge yourself between a few rocks to pull yourself up to the next level. Then proceed up the rock slab next to the falls. During various times of the year it can be wet, so proceed with great caution. Once at the top of this area you will have to cross over a few logs to make it to the top of the ledge.

This is not really a place for kids or older people. A great place though for teens and those who like to rock climb!

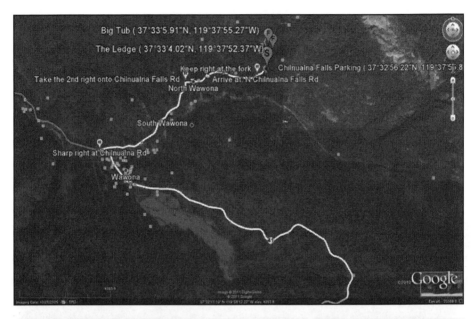

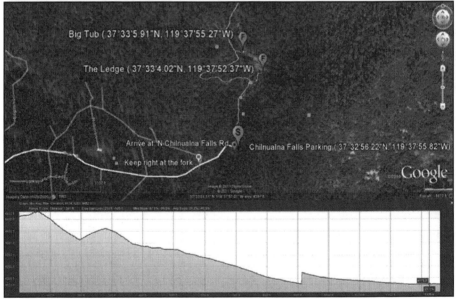

THE LEDGE

LONG CANYON

Big Meadow Campground (off of Hell Hole Rd)
Access: Hike 0.25 miles one way (0.5 miles round trip)
Level: Easy

Bathrooms nearby: Yes
Water Temperature: Moderate
Clothing Optional: No
Dog/Kid friendly: Yes
Best Season: Good to visit all year round

If Long Canyon were a lady, she would have the perfect hour-glass figure. This swimming hole has perfect lines in almost every way. A perfect kidney-shaped pool is fed by a 10-foot falls. The pool is about 45 feet long on its major axis and is on the same plane as the water flow. The deep end of the pool is about 8 to 10 feet and is furthest away from the small falls and water chute. The best jumping spot is closest to the falls. However, the water is only about 4 to 5 feet deep at that place in the swimming hole. The falls is formed by a long channel or chute that can be used as a killer water slide. It's very popular with kids and is one of the best components of Long Canyon.

There are a few small tubs below the main Long Canyon pool. Both the vertical and horizontal elements of this swimming hole would be considered fair. No real great jumping spots, but a few good places to drop a towel and relax.

The expectation of privacy is fairly low given the close proximity of the campground.

The trail getting down to the swimming hole is fairly well worn and flat until you reach the last 30 yards. The last 30 yards to the swimming hole are steep, but most young children should be able to make it fairly easily.

Restaurant and Bathrooms:

The closest bathrooms are at the Big Meadow Campground.

Information and Contact:

There is no fee here. For additional photos, please visit our website at: http://swimmingholesofcalifornia.blogspot.com

Highlights

You can take the kids and the entire family to this swimming hole. Not many places for junior to get into trouble. Bring a blanket and picnic basket and spend the day with that special person watching the falls. Some campers like to swim here after dark.

LONG CANYON

LONG CANYON

LONG CANYON

LONG CANYON

Driving Directions:

Drive east on Wentworth Springs Rd. (paved) to Eleven Pines Rd. (24 miles). Follow Eleven Pines Rd. to Hell Hole Rd. (19 miles). Then stay right until the Big Meadow Campground which will be on your right. If you get lost just go the campground (Big Meadow Campground). This is basically a campground swimming hole. There is a concrete bridge that water runs across as you enter the campground. Continue past this bridge. At the campground just park and walk toward the river. Follow the worn trail to the swimming hole. It's not far. It's about 150 yards down from a small dam station. The road to the campground is in good condition and can be easily driven using a regular automobile.

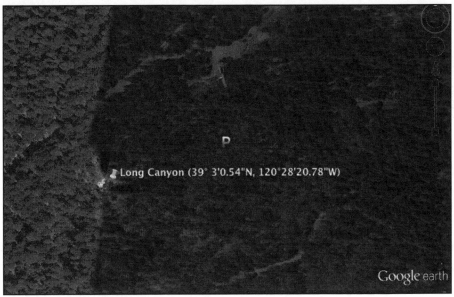

LITTLE HAWAII

Yosemite National Forest off Hwy. 49
Access: Hike 0.5 miles one way (1.0 miles round trip)
Level: Easy
Bathrooms nearby: Yes

Water Temperature: Cold
Clothing Optional: Yes, lower tubs
Dog/Kid friendly: No
Best Season: July & August

A series of falls all stacked on top of each other like a beautiful wedding cake. Plant life and elephant ears are abundant about the swimming hole. There are lots of separate tubs and pools to swim and play in. The top two holes are the most frequently visited. The first is a 15-foot falls that goes into a nice pool. Later in the year, the falls can act as a nice water slide. The second hole is slightly wider, about 45 feet long, but with very limited seating on steep slabs. This is not really a kid friendly place, but is ideal for a couple. The best privacy is at the lower holes and falls and would be rated good to excellent.

Bonus Feature:

You get to cross the Wawona Golf Course. If the road is closed you can always rent a bike and ride to the bridge over Big Creek.

Restaurant and Bathrooms:

The closest bathrooms are at the Wawona Inn. There is a gas station and a restaurant at the Wawona Inn which is less than a mile away from the swimming hole.

Information and Contact:

There is a fee to enter Yosemite Park.

For additional photos, please visit our website at:

http://swimmingholesofcalifornia.blogspot.com

Highlights

Plan ahead and stay overnight at the Wawona. There are places to BBQ and play golf nearby.

Driving Directions:

From Oakhurst drive north on SR 41 and enter Yosemite Park. There is an entrance fee, unless you opt to get the annual pass (which is a good idea if you go to swimming holes regularly). Turn left at the entrance and head toward the Wawona. Turn left at the road across from the Wawona (Chowchilla Rd.) and drive across the golf course. Watch for flying golf balls!

Stay on this road for about 2 miles. The road is dirt and slightly narrow and steep in sections. Continue on this road until you reach a bridge that crosses Big Creek. There is a small parking area on the other side of the bridge that can accommodate a few cars.

The trail is on the left side of the creek if you look down river from the bridge. The trail is not easy to spot and proceeds parallel to the creek for about 0.5 miles. Follow the trail down until it reaches an area near the creek. The swimming hole is at the bottom of the falls.

Stanislaus National Forest, off Hwy. 120 near Yosemite
Access: Hike 0.25 miles one way (0.5 miles round trip)
Elevation: Starts at 3100 feet; total loss of 50 feet
Level: Easy

Bathrooms nearby: Yes
Water Temperature: Cold
Clothing Optional: No
Dog/Kid friendly: Yes
Best Season: July-September/Early spring the water is too cold and the falls are too powerful

If you don't mind sharing and rubbing elbows with the locals, then Rainbow Pool Falls will be one of your favorite swimming holes. Rainbow Pool Falls is a combination 20-foot waterfall and swimming hole located on Hwy. 120 in the Stanislaus National Forest just about 20 miles from the Big Oak Flat entrance to Yosemite.

This is the perfect place to take the kids when Yosemite is too crowded. Rainbow Pool Falls is a river waterfall. That means that the falls are made from a giant rock impound that spans the entire width of the river. Further, this means that the falls can be very powerful in the spring and will continue to run even into the late fall.

The falls feed down into a giant swimming hole which is probably around 50 yards wide as it's long. There is also a nice beach area for putting down some lawn chairs to watch the swimmers jump, dive, slide, and wade around the falls.

It's no surprise that Rainbow Pool Falls is popular with teenagers. Many like to try their luck by jumping off the high cliff. Others who are more careful will slide down the granite chute which is next to the waterfall. Later in the year when the falls slow down, some people have been known to swim under the falls to an air pocket located behind the falls.

As to opposed to other places up the street in Yosemite, where the water is really cold, the water here at Rainbow Pool Falls is more moderate. This is another bonus of a drive up falls like this one.

If you are looking for privacy, there are a few better options if you follow the trail to the right of the fall near the dam up the river a short distance.

Restaurant and Bathrooms:

The closest bathrooms are at the falls. Closest restaurants are about 5 miles away or in Groveland.

Information and Contact:

There is no fee here. For a map and more information visit website www.fs.fed.us/r5/maps/ or Stanislaus National Forest, Groveland Ranger District, 24545 Hwy. 120, Groveland, CA 95321, 209/962-7825,

For additional photos, please visit our website at:

http://swimmingholesofcalifornia.blogspot.com

Highlights

If you like jumping from cliffs and don't like to hike, this is the place for you. This is a great place to stop if you are heading to Yosemite.

RAINBOW POOL FALLS

RAINBOW POOL FALLS

Driving Directions

From Groveland, drive east on Hwy. 120 for about 13 miles (toward Yosemite National Park), until you reach the bridge over the South Fork of the Tuolumne River. The turn off is on the right-hand side before you cross the bridge. The road is paved and it goes down for about 0.5 miles to the falls. If you see the road to Cherry Lake/Sweetwater Camp, on the left, then you have gone too far.

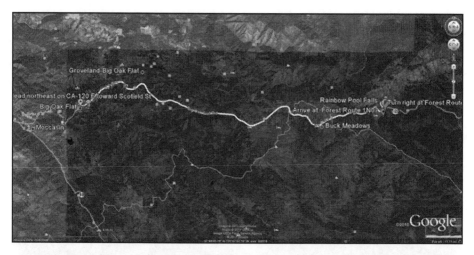

Yosemite National Forest off Hwy. 49 (Big Sandy Rd.)
Access: Hike 0.25 miles one way (0.5 miles round trip)
Level: Easy

Bathrooms nearby: Yes
Water Temperature: Cold
Clothing Optional: Yes, lower tubs
Dog/Kid friendly: Yes
Best Season: Good all year round

Here is a swimming hole that is popular, yet does not see too much traffic. A broad cascade empties into a few shallow pools about 40 feet wide. Below this pool is the main falls and swimming area. The main falls is about 30 feet high with walls that enclose the swimming hole in almost 180 degrees. The water is held in a 40-foot diameter pool by a 6-foot rock impound carved out of the granite.

Both the vertical and horizontal elements are excellent. This swimming hole has plenty of places to jump on almost all sides. The pool is plenty deep at more than 10 feet in places. Many people like to cross at the top of the falls. The author spoke with a few locals who relayed a story that their uncle one year slipped and went over the edge of the falls. Lucky there were no injuries. Be very careful here! Many of the locals jump from the top of the falls all the time. The real high divers like the 40- to 50-foot jumps on the other side of the swimming hole. If you are adventurous there is a secret sitting place behind the falls. It can fit roughly 3 to 4 people. The hard part is getting up the slippery rocks to the underside of the falls. Skinny Dip is a great place to relax on a hot day or hang out with some friends.

This swimming hole has almost everything to offer except for a slide. The road is a little rough getting to the swimming hole. It's mostly dirt with some rocks and bumps, but passable with most standard automobiles.

Locating the trail down to the swimming hole is not very easy. However, once you are on the trail it's straight forward getting there.

Skinny Dip has largely been considered a secret swimming hole of locals. However, it has recently seen more traffic with the Tenaya Lodge nearby. The name is a misnomer. No skinny-dipping going on here. There is an opportunity down river about 100 years at a place called Arrow Head. That is clothing optional.

Bonus Feature:

There are plenty of places to rent mountain bikes nearby. This is the best way to travel up Big Sandy Rd.

Restaurant and Bathrooms:

The closest bathrooms and restaurants are at the Tenaya Lodge or just off of Hwy. 49.

Information and Contact:

There is no charge to enter this area. Please note that if you have any questions or emergencies, the point of contact is the Mi-Wuk Ranger Station.

For additional photos and a video, please visit our website at:

http://swimmingholesofcalifornia.blogspot.com

Highlights

This is a teenage local hangout place on summer weekends.

SKINNY DIP

SKINNY DIP

Driving Directions:

From Oakhurst drive north on SR 41 to Fish Camp, California. Turn right at Big Sandy Rd. (a.k.a. Jackson Rd.) just before the Tenaya Lodge. Follow the dirt road to the right and continue for about a mile through a gate. The road is dirt and starts to narrow. It will continue along a cliff. Drive another 1.0 miles up the hill for a total of 3.5 miles from Rt. 41. Skinny Dip is a little difficult to locate, but the GPS coordinates (listed on the map) should be correct. On Big Sandy Rd. there is a small pull off on the right just before the road banks to the left. The trail down to the river is covered over by some tree branches. It's right over a small drain pipe. You can't see the drain pipe easily, unless you traverse over the side of the road slightly. It's about 0.25 miles down to the hole once you start down the trail.

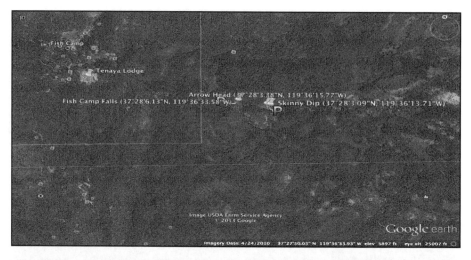

THE BIG TUB

Yosemite National Forest off Hwy. 49
Access: Hike 1.0 miles one way (2 miles round trip)
Level: Easy

Bathrooms nearby: Yes
Water Temperature: Cold
Clothing Optional: No, private pool
Dog/Kid friendly: Yes
Best Season: July & August

A giant beautiful tub carved out of granite is fed by a 15-foot falls. The tub is about 20 feet in diameter with smooth geometric contours. Plenty of places to layout and catch some rays and a sun tan. There are a number of really neat bucket seats to the left of the tub just below the falls. The tub is a good 10- to 12-feet deep. It's a nice little jump from the right side.

The tub and falls are not easy to find. I've known of many people hiking up and down the Chilnualna trail looking for the Big Tub to no avail. In a sense it's the perfect hidden swimming hole. This swimming hole is right off of the Chilnualna Trail. However, miraculously it maintains a certain amount of privacy because it's behind a large boulder that shelters its approach.

If you try to swim at The Big Tub too early in the year or during the Spring you will find it unapproachable and the tubs completely submerged under water. Too late in the year such as September and the pools can become stagnant.

Restaurant and Bathrooms:

The closest bathrooms are at the base of the Chilnualna Trail. There is a gas station and a restaurant at the Wawona Inn which is less than a mile away.

Information and Contact:

There is a fee to enter Yosemite Park.

For additional photos and a video, please visit our website at:

http://swimmingholesofcalifornia.blogspot.com

Highlights

Plan ahead and stay overnight at the Wawona. There are places to BBQ and play golf nearby.

Driving Directions

From Oakhurst drive north on SR 41 and enter Yosemite Park. There is an entrance fee, unless you opt to get the annual pass (which is a good idea if you go to swimming holes regularly). Turn left at the entrance and head toward the Wawona. Take the first right onto Chilnualna Rd. just past the Wawona. It's about 1.5 miles on this road. It's a little tricky because it winds through a number of cabins. The trailhead parking is not so clear. It's right next to the bathrooms. If you get to a small bridge that crosses the creek, you have gone too far.

The trail has a small metal sign marking the path just to the left of the creek. There are two hiking options. The first is to follow the trail along the creek to the right. The other is to stay left of the trail and pick up the trail as it circles back to the left from the creek. It might be best to first take the trail along the creek to learn the trail and where you can pick it up.

The trail along the creek might not be suitable for small children since it becomes quite steep in places. Just along the lower falls there are a series of granite steps up the steep cliff.

The trail then comes to an end and with a switchback to the left. There is a little section here that you need to carefully traverse to proceed up the trail to the junction. The junction has a number of trail names listed with options.

The trail proceeds away from the creek and then makes a switchback and again heads toward the creek. You will be getting close when you begin to proceed up the trail and start to parallel the creek again.

It's very easy to miss the trail down to the creek. If you exit the trail too early you will find yourself looking over a cliff down on Honeymooner's and The Ledge swimming holes. If you exit too later you will miss the swimming hole and not be able to access the creek.

Follow the small trail down to the creek. You will not be able to see The Big Tub since the view is blocked by a large boulder placed by God to maintain privacy.

You can proceed up the creek to the left or later in the year cross over the creek to the right. Water shoes would be a good option.

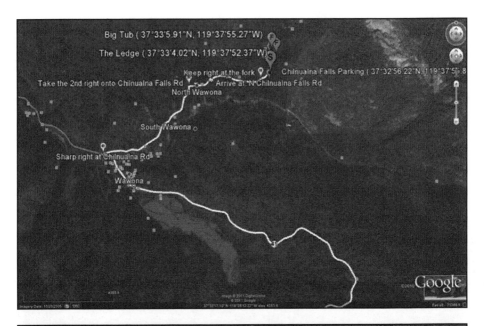

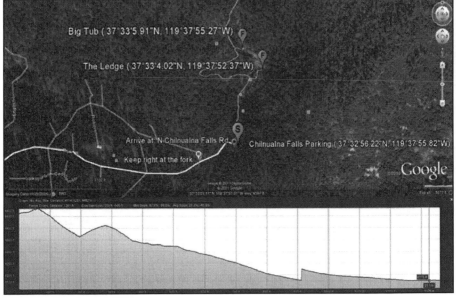

TUB CITY

Stanislaus National Forest, off Sonora Hwy. 108 near Long Barn
Access: Hike 0.25 miles one way (0.5 miles round trip)
Level: Easy

Bathrooms nearby: No
Water Temperature: Cold
Clothing Optional: Yes
Dog/Kid friendly: Yes
Best Season: August & September/Best time for the tubs is early September

In June 1967, the Beatles made a statement on their latest long playing record: "I read the news today oh boy, Four thousand holes in Blackburn, Lancashire, And though the holes were rather small, They had to count them all Now they know how many holes it takes to fill the Albert Hall."

Similarly, we could make such great music and ask the same question regarding Tub City. How many holes are there in Tub City? Answer: Too many to count, but just enough to enjoy!

Tub City is a beautiful falls and series of tubs that line almost 1 mile of granite on the upper Clavey River. If you don't like your tub, just move to another. No real vertical element here, but there is a nice water slide at the bottom of the granite slabs. There also are some larger tubs near the middle of Tub City that look more like an infinity pool. This is a good

TUB CITY

swimming hole to visit later in the year. It stays flowing even after many other places go stagnant. The road getting to Tub City is dirt and can get rough in a few places. Four-wheel drive and a truck are recommended.

The expectation of privacy here is quite good. Particularly in September after most of the kids have gone back to school and the tubs are still running. Don't forget to look for the stone arch on top of one of the boulders. A clever person decided to stack stones in such a way as to make an arch. It's been there for quite some time.

Restaurant and Bathrooms:

The closest bathrooms and restaurants are in Mi-Wuk or Long Barn.

Information and Contact:

There is no fee here. For further information please contact the Mi-Wuk Ranger Station.

For additional photos, please visit our website at:

http://swimmingholesofcalifornia.blogspot.com

Highlights

This is a great swimming hole to hit at the end of the summer when all the other swimming holes are stagnant. The best time to visit Tub City is in the beginning of September.

TUB CITY

TUB CITY

Driving Directions:

From Mi-Wuk Village, head southeast on CA 108 E/Sonora Pass Hwy. toward Sierra Park Rd. (11.9 miles). Turn right on Crabtree Rd. Continue straight on FS 4N11 (223 ft.). Turn right at Forest Route 4N25 and go 3.2 miles, continue on Crabtree Rd. (FS 4N26) another 5.0 miles. Turn left to stay on FR 4N25. Go 2.0 miles and then turn left on FS 4N09. Go 0.5 miles and then take the 1st right onto FS 3N29. Arrive at the bridge over the Clavey River. Hike down the river or the road for about 1.0 miles until you reach Tub City.

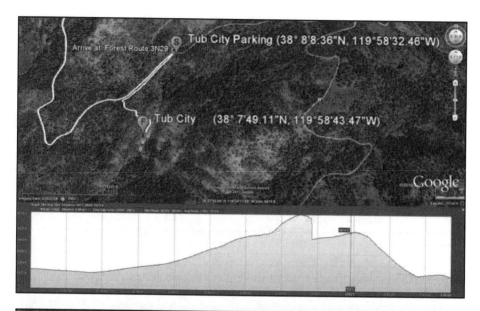

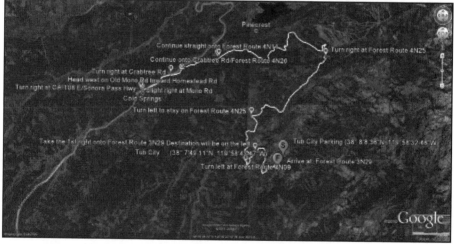

TUB CITY

★ TUOLUMNE RIVER & PRESTON FALLS

Stanislaus National Forest, off of Hwy. 120 near Groveland
Access: Hike 0.25 miles one way (0.5 miles round trip)
Elevation: Starts at 2,400 feet; total gain 500ft
Level: Moderate

Water Temperature: Moderate
Clothing Optional: Yes, at falls
Dog/Kid friendly: Yes
Best Season: Summer and Fall

The Tuolumne River has been designated a Wild and Scenic River, under the 1968 California Wild and Scenic Rivers Act. The Act provides that rivers possessing extraordinary scenic, recreational, fishery, or wildlife values shall be preserved in their free-flowing state, together with their immediate environments, for the benefit and enjoyment of the people of the state. The Tuolumne was added to the Wild and Scenic Rivers System on September 28, 1984.

The name for the Tuolumne River (twah'-luh-me) has as many possible meanings as it does spellings. The original meaning of the word "Tuolumne" may have been "cave people" or "stone wigwams," both taken from the history of tribes known as "Taulamnell," or "Tahualamne," or

Yokuts Indians living near Knights Ferry in the rocks and recesses by the river. Another theory is that "Tuolumne" is derived from a Central Sierra Miwok word "talmalmne," whose meaning is unclear today.

The Tuolomne River has some of the best swimming holes in the state of California. The hard part is deciding which one to visit first. We list two great swimming holes here. If you are adventurous you could probably find one of your own.

The first swimming hole is about 1.5 miles from the trailhead. It comprises an awesome amphitheater of rock and granite rising in some places up to 60 feet in height. Water pours down a few falls into a small channel. The channel runs for more than 100 yards. There are a few pools formed through the channel that range from 30 to 40 feet wide. The pools that are formed make great areas for jumping from the rocks on both sides of the river.

There are some seating ledges and a large slanted rock that provides the perfect trajectory for a small rope swing that has been constructed over the wide pool. The pools here are all very deep (20 feet or more in some places).

There are lots of Black Oak trees that line this swimming hole. They provide for the right amount of shade if one wants to relax on the slabs that align next to the river.

Further up the river (4.4 miles from the trailhead, or another 2.5 miles from the first swimming hole) is Preston Falls. This is a beautiful 15-foot falls that plunges down into a wide swimming area over at least 100 yards in length. The best places for sunbathing are going to be on the ledge at the left side of the falls (as you face them). This is a great place for nude sunbathers, because you can't get to this ledge easily without wading in the river. Also, the ledge is not easily viewed from the trail. However, from the ledge it's easy to view someone coming up the trail. The ledge slants at about a 30 degree angle to the water and has a rock barrier that creates privacy.

There is a rock that juts out just next to the falls. It provides the perfect diving board. Just be careful here because the river flow is strong. It can be fun in the summer to jump into the water and float down stream. Don't try this in the spring if you know what is good for you.

The canyon and trail to Preston Falls is like a desert during the summer. Be prepared by bringing extra water and take frequent dips in the river on the way. At one point, you will encounter a grassy field with beautiful wild flowers which you have to cross. Having boots might be a good option here. However, if you hike this trail in the summer heat, it would be unlikely that you would encounter any snakes. Take care to leave enough time for the hike back.

The trail travels 4.4 miles up the north side of the Tuolumne River on a moderately undulating grade. You will know when you are near the falls because you will encounter the remains of an old cabin and chimney. An early explorer named Preston built the cabin that was probably destroyed by the Cave Diggings Fire of 1928, and the 1937 flood.

In summary, two awesome swimming holes that include everything you could ever want; great jumps, beautiful falls, high granite walls, clean water, and a rope swing.

Restaurant and Bathrooms:

The closest bathrooms are at the trailhead parking area. The closet restaurant is at the Evergreen Lodge.

Information and Contact:

There is no fee here.

For additional photos, please visit our website at:

http://swimmingholesofcalifornia.blogspot.com

Highlights

Stop at the Evergreen lodge to gather snacks and eat lunch. They have some good vegan selections.

TUOLUMNE RIVER & PRESTON FALLS

Driving Directions:

From Groveland, drive east on Hwy. 120 for 14 miles toward Yosemite. Turn left on Cherry Lake Rd. and Sweet Water Camp. Follow the road past the Evergreen Lodge and toward Mather. Instead of going toward Mather, bear left at the intersection and continue on the same road (FS1S02). Follow this along the cliff above the Tuolumne River (it should be on your right) for about 1.0 miles until you come to a steep road toward the power plant. Follow this down for a total of 7.8 miles until you reach the trailhead beyond the power plant. Park and follow the trail up river for about 1.5 miles to the first swimming hole and another 2.8 miles to Preston Falls.

YOSEMITE CREEK

Stanislaus National Forest, off of Hwy. 120 near Groveland
Access: Hike 0.25 miles one way (0.5 miles round trip)
Elevation: Starts at 2,400 feet; total gain 500ft
Level: Moderate

Bathrooms nearby: Yes
Water Temperature: Moderate
Clothing Optional: Yes, at falls
Dog/Kid friendly: Yes
Best Season: July, August, & September

Yosemite Creek forms a perfect equilateral triangle as it enters this swimming hole. The deepest end of the swimming hole is at the apex of the triangle and then it becomes much shallower at the base. The water is cold even on the hottest August days, and the pool is about 10 to 15 feet deep at the deep end. There is plenty of shade and trees around the swimming hole. Further, there is a nice sandy ramp for entering the water at the deep end.

There is a pretty good vertical element also. The cliffs around the pool are around 15 to 20 feet, with the best point for jumping being closest to the apex and deep side of the swimming hole.

We found the expectation of privacy to be pretty good here. This is a popular hiking trail for people staying at Yosemite Campground down below. However, the swimming hole is not easy to spot from the trail. It took us about an hour to boulder hop up the creek to finally locate the pool. For this reason, it's unlikely that hikers would just stumble into Yosemite Creek, unless they knew it was there.

Early in the season, the water runs quite rapid down through the rocks prior to entering the broader pool. The water actually enters the pool at a right angle to the apex of the triangle. There are a number of tubs and possible slides located in this area.

Restaurant and Bathrooms:

The closest bathrooms are at the trailhead parking area.

Information and Contact:

There is no fee here.

For additional photos, please visit our website at:

http://swimmingholesofcalifornia.blogspot.com

Highlights

Yosemite Campground is not far away. You can start there and hike up the trail. The trail is not too steep and can accommodate mountain bikes.

Driving Directions:

From Sonora drive south on SR 49, 14.5 miles to SR 120. Drive east 68 long winding miles to SR 41, and continue another 19 miles on SR 120 (Tioga Pass) until you reach the parking for Yosemite Creek and the Ten Lakes Trail. Descend 0.75 miles to a creek. Cross the creek and hike parallel down the creek for another 0.25 miles until you reach the swimming hole. The previous picture provides an idea regarding when you should leave the trail and cut across the creek.

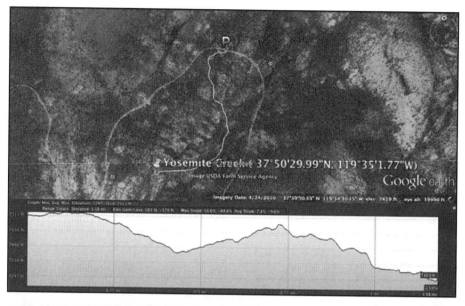

THE SEQUOIAS

BUCKEYE FLAT, THE BRIDGE, KAWEAH FALLS & PARADISE CREEK

Sequoia National Park, off Hwy. 198 near Three Rivers and the Buckeye Campground
Access: Hike 0.25 miles one way (0.5 miles round trip)
Level: Easy

Bathrooms nearby: Yes, at the Buckeye Campground Sequoia National Park, off Hwy. 198 near Three Rivers and the Buckeye Campground
Water Temperature: Moderate/Cold
Clothing Optional: No
Dog/Kid friendly: Yes
Best Season: July & August
Note: All these swimming holes are fairly close to each other so they are listed together

Given the close proximity of these four swimming holes we've listed them all together. The first swimming hole you will encounter will be Buckeye Flat. This is located just past campsite #28 as you round the corner in the road.

Buckeye Flat has a nice rope swing and rock slide slightly further up the river. From time to time the locals set up a zip line that runs from the opposing bank of the river over the swimming area. This is not encouraged by the ranger service. Buckeye Flat is a great swimming area for the little dippers. There is a nice sandy beach and trees that provide shade for pulling up a lawn chair and relaxing.

On the other side of the road at campsite #28 is a trail that leads up into the woods and then back down to the river. If you follow this trail for about 0.5 miles, you will come to a beautiful bridge. The swimming hole is just under this bridge. Teenagers like to jump off the 20-foot bridge into the river. This is not recommended and only possible early in the year. There are sandy beaches on both sides of the river.

If you continue on and cross the bridge you will come to a fork in the trail. If you go right you will go to Paradise Creek Falls. If you go left you will go to Kaweah Falls (also known as "Little Niagra" by the locals). Both are only about 0.25 miles. The great thing about this area is if the water is running too fast on the Kaweah river you can always head to the calmer and more peaceful waters of Paradise Creek. If it's late in the year and Paradise Creek is nearly dried up, you can head to Kaweah Falls and slide down the falls like most of the locals. This is not for the faint of heart though since the falls are about 25 feet high. However, it's great fun! Jumps are possible at all the swimming holes. Paradise Creek is about 8 to 10 feet deep at its base. Kaweah Falls is at least 20 feet at its base. The bridge can vary depending upon the time of year. Buckeye Flat varies in depth depending upon where you swim in the river.

So if you are not sure where to go, you might want to head out to Buckeye Flat and the other swimming holes. They have everything you could ever want. Further, if you decide that you want to stay at the campground you should note that it's not done on a reservation system. Campsites are allocated on a first-come, first-serve basis. I heard one local tell me this was one of the best things about the camping. He had been coming to the place for more than 17 years and would not have been able to do that if the park service changed the system to be by lottery or reservation.

In summary, a great place for a family vacation and to relax. Note that in some books they mention the option of driving and parking in dirt pullouts near Buckeye Flat. This is no longer an option and all day use hikers must park back at Hospital Rock and hike the 1.2 miles of road to the campground. This is no big issue. The road to Buckeye Flat is quite narrow and in many places can only accommodate one car. In contrast, the cliff the road runs along is quite high and steep. You probably don't want to drive on this road anyways. The views are pretty nice, so why not enjoy a short hike before you reach camp!

Last, there is a fifth swimming hole down a short trail as you head up the road to Buckeye Flat. This trail leads to "Indian Head." It's a short hike down that stops at the river. It's paved most of the way, and one can be easily mislead into thinking that the trail will take you to the campground. The trail ends at a nice little swimming hole with a falls. This swimming hole is probably best visited late in the year given the power of the river in this area. The giant rock and falls give a similar feel and impression of the Candy Rock swimming hole located in Sonora, California.

Given the ease of access to the swimming hole, privacy is unlikely.

Restaurant and Bathrooms:

There are bathrooms at Buckeye Flat, the parking area near Hospital Rock, and at the Ranger Station just down the hill.

Information and Contact:

There is a fee to enter this area. For a map of Sequoia National Forest, contact the office below or visit the website at www.fs.fed.us/r5/maps/. For further information please contact Sequoia National Forest, Hwy. 198, Springville, CA 93265, 559-539-2607, website: www.r5.fs.fed.us/sequoia.

For additional photos and a video, please visit our website at:

http://swimmingholesofcalifornia.blogspot.com

Highlights

Plan ahead and stay overnight at the Hampton Inn in Visalia and Tulare. There are a number of swimming holes in close proximity. The Cliffs is a great swimming hole nearby. Further up the same road is Morro Rock.

BUCKEYE FLAT, THE BRIDGE, KAWEAH FALLS & PARADISE CREEK

Driving Directions:

From Visalia, drive east on Hwy. 198 for 47 miles to the turnoff on the right to Buckeye Flat Campground, across from Hospital Rock. Park at the parking lot on the left across from Hospital Rock. Walk up the road about 0.6 miles until you reach the campground area. To reach Kaweah Falls, The Bridge, and Paradise Creek, look for site #28 on the left and follow the trail toward the river. For the Buckeye Flat swimming hole proceed to the campsite on the corner as the road turns to the right. Follow the trail down until the river. To reach The Bridge continue on the trail until you reach the Kaweah River. The Bridge crosses the river and the swimming hole is downstream. Continue across the bridge and toward the right about 0.25 miles to reach Paradise Creek and Falls. Continue to the left for about 0.25 miles to reach Kaweah Falls, a.k.a. "Little Niagra."

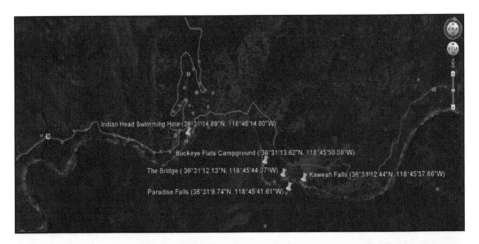

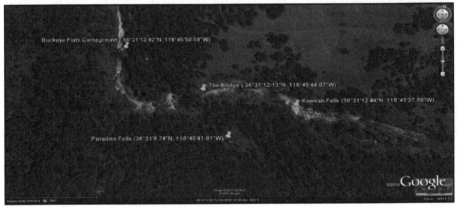

⭐5 GALENA CREEK & HIDDEN FALLS

Mountain Home Demonstration State Forest off Hwy. 190 near Springville
Access: Hike 0.25 miles round trip to Hidden Falls and 1.5 miles round trip to Galena Creek
Elevation: Starts at 5900 feet; total loss of 30 feet to Hidden Falls, and 100 ft to Galena Creek

Level: Easy
Bathrooms nearby: Yes
Water Temperature: Moderate
Clothing Optional: No
Dog/Kid friendly: Yes
Best Season: July & August, all year round to view falls

No swimming hole book would be complete without including Galena Creek and Hidden Falls. However, to be honest with you these are not really swimming holes. They are beautiful places to visit and photograph, but not user friendly. We aren't saying that they aren't worth visiting either. This is more of a place to visit while you are camping. It's a nice place to take a dip and cool off if you are already visiting one of the campgrounds. It's not a place to plan a day trip with a group of friends to visit a swimming hole. There are some good reasons for this.

Getting to Hidden Falls is a long drive. We mean a really long drive. It's in the Mountain Home Demonstration State Forest, 22 long miles from Springfield. Ever heard of it?

The road getting there is steep, narrow, winding, and can take at least an hour to ascend. Make sure that you follow the directions exactly for you don't want to miss the turn and end up taking Balch Park Rd. all the way to Hidden Falls. It's one of the worst roads in the Sierras.

Once you get to the state forest you will notice the road splits. If you go to the left you will proceed down to an open space area with a small lake and camping areas. The turn to the right takes you to Hidden Falls and Galena Creek.

This is a very interesting place given that there are so many large sequoias and redwood trees outside the national park area. We recommend that you pick up a map at the park headquarters. It's easy to get lost here.

It's about 6 miles to get down to Hidden Falls and Galena Creek. The road is narrow, steep, and dirt in most areas. It's passable using a standard automobile in late fall. It's not clear what the quality of this road is like in a wet spring. Given the amount of mud, we would say difficult.

You will first reach Hidden Falls. Hidden Falls is a walk-in camp. Day hikers park in a different lot above the campground. Therefore, if you are there to just visit the falls, there should be adequate parking.

The interesting thing about Hidden Falls is that they really are hidden. You will be right on top of them and not even know where they are. They are located down river from the road. Just follow the steep path down to the creek. Still can't see the falls? Yeah, you will actually have to get down into the river to get the full show. The best viewing and photographing point is on the other side of the river in front of or on top of the large fallen Sequoia tree trunk.

The total height of the falls is about 50 feet. The falls descend gradually with the steepest portion being at the end of a schist chute which has a drop of about 20 feet to a fan-shaped pool. The falls are best viewed at high flow times. The pool at the base of the falls comprises lots of cobble and depth can vary based on the time of year and overall level of rain fall. At high water we would anticipate the pool to get up to 2 or 3 feet deep. However, most of the time it's going to be much shallower, because there is no rock impound. Most people prefer to swim in some of the deeper pools upstream on the other side of the road. The expectation of privacy would be considered quite low here because of the hikers, proximity to the road, and campers in the area.

If you drove all the way to Hidden Falls, you might as well continue a little further for about 2 miles to the Moses Gulch Campground and visit Galena Creek. When you reach the Moses Gulch Campground, you will be at the end of the road. Park near the bathrooms and head down the road (a fork) toward campsites 6-10 until you reach the River Trail which will cross the road. It's not easy to find. It's about 0.75 miles to Galena Creek from the campsites. Basically, you will follow the trail down 0.25 miles to the river. The fun part begins when you cross the river. There are various ways of doing this. Most people appear to cross via a large worn tree trunk that is up about 12 feet above the river. Other options are available.

Once you reach the other side of the river, it's a mostly flat hike down to Galena Creek. It's about 0.5 miles until you arrive. When we visited the area, there were lots of people playing in the creek and woods just above Galena Creek. Most of the people were surprised to find out that there was an actual waterfall there! The trail crosses a small stream or channel just before you arrive. There is a small spur trail leading down to the creek. It basically is right at the point where the trail begins to turn away from the creek and begins to ascend.

Be careful getting down to the creek. The rocks can be slippery and are not so user friendly. Galena Creek is different from many falls because it comprises almost 180 degrees of waterfalls cascading down about 20 feet and all feeding into a narrow tub of about 15 feet wide and 30 feet long. There is ample ledge space for viewing the falls and relaxing. Still further down is a deeper pool you can bob up and down in at the deep end. The expectation of privacy is pretty good here.

Restaurant and Bathrooms:

The closest bathrooms are at park headquarters or the Moses Gulch Campground entrance for Galena Creek.

Information and Contact:

There is no fee here. A free map of the Mountain Home Demonstration

State Forest is available at the park headquarters (See directions below).

For more information, contact Mountain Home Demonstration State Forest, P.O. Box 517, Springville, CA 93265, 559/539-2321 (summer).

Highlights

This is a great place for photographing some unique waterfalls.

GALENA CREEK & HIDDEN FALLS

Driving Directions:

From Porterville, drive east on Hwy. 190 for 18 miles to Springville. At Springville, bear left at the fork, turn left (north) on Balch Park Rd./Rd. 239 and drive 3.5 miles, then turn right on Bear Creek Rd./Rd. 220. Drive 14 miles to Mountain Home State Park. Stop at the Headquarters and pick up a map. They are free. Continue 0.75 miles on Bear Creek Rd. and turn right. Drive two miles and turn right, then drive 1.5 miles and turn left for Hidden Falls and Right for Galena Creek. Hidden Falls Campground is 0.25 miles further. For Galena Creek, drive one mile to the Moses Gulch Campground. Take the road and fork toward campsites 6-10.

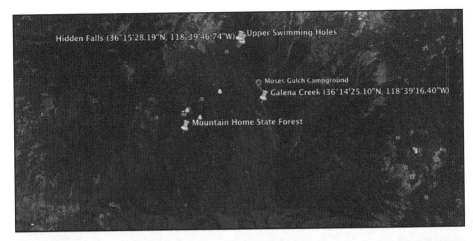

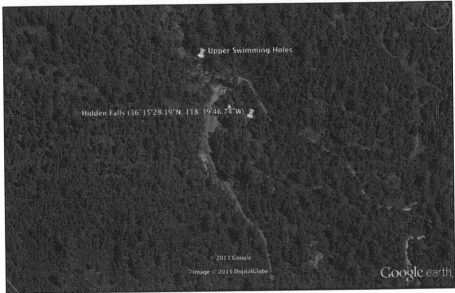

LILY'S LAGOON/ STEVENSON GULLY

Giant Sequoia National Monument, off Hwy. 190 near Springville
Access: Hike 0.25 miles one way (0.5 miles round trip)
Level: Easy

Bathrooms nearby: Yes in Springville there is a park in the center of town with restrooms
Water Temperature: Cold
Clothing Optional: Yes
Dog/Kid friendly: No
Best Season: July & August
Note: Although the hike is fairly easy, the location is at about 3000 feet elevation

The Middle Fork Tule River has some spectacular waterfalls and swimming holes. One of the best and easiest to access stretches of the Tule features this amazing swimming hole with small falls and side lagoon.

Radiant and clear water circles all around from the small falls at the base of a large triangular shaped swimming hole. It's a pale aquamarine color with cattail and peppermint at the base. Ledges are about 10 to 15 feet high and provide for the best access to the water.

There are ample ledges to catch some rays and some limited Manzanitas that provide shade along the river. The swimming hole is clearly visible from the trail coming down. So privacy is somewhat limited in the main pool. However, adjoining the main pool is a small lagoon that is neither visible from above nor when standing on the nearby ledges. This makes for an excellent place to take a date to enjoy the day. There is a nice ledge and rocks adjoining the lagoon with shade provided by the nearby trees. The lagoon is about 3 to 4 feet in places and protected by a small rock ledge. This provides ample opportunity for clothing optional participants.

This area and canyon can get quite hot. When we visited the temperature was about 112 degrees F. Bring extra water and plan accordingly since you are at reasonably high altitude.

Restaurant and Bathrooms:

The closest bathrooms are at the park located in the center of Springville, California.

Information and Contact:

There is a fee to enter this area. For a map of Sequoia National Forest, contact the office below or visit the website at www.fs.fed.us/r5/maps/. For further information please contact Giant Sequoia National Monument/Sequoia National Forest, Tule River Ranger District, 32588 Hwy. 190, Springville, CA 93265, 559-539-2607, website: www.r5.fs.fed.us/sequoia.

For additional photos and a video, please visit our website at:

http://swimmingholesofcalifornia.blogspot.com

Highlights

Plan ahead and stay overnight at the Hampton Inn in Tulare. California Hot Springs is just up the road if you are interested in spending a day at a hot springs also. There are also a number of other swimming holes nearby and easy to access.

LILY'S LAGOON/ STEVENSON GULLY

Driving Directions:

From Porterville, drive east on Hwy. 190 for 18 miles to Springville. From Springville, continue on Hwy. 190 for 7.5 miles until you reach the powerhouse bridge and the exit to Camp Wishon and Wishon Dr. (Rd. 208). Cross the bridge and continue straight on Hwy. 190 up the mountain on the winding road for another 1.7 miles. The turn off will be on the right. Prior to the turnoff there is a view of the falls that is easy to miss. This will help given you an idea of the location. There is a forest service sign at the turnoff parking area. The trail is located to the right of the forest service sign at the bottom right side of the turnoff. The trail you will be hiking on is the Stevenson Trail. It is a somewhat well maintained and good trail. Follow it down until you come to a fork. Follow the fork and switchbacks to the left and down. If you do, you will reach Lily's Lagoon. You will know you are on the right trail almost immediately since you will get a view of Lily's Lagoon (a.k.a. Stevenson Gully) from the trail.

☆ MIDDLE FORK TULE RIVER FALLS

Giant Sequoia National Monument, off Hwy. 190 near Springville
Access: Hike 0.25 miles one way (0.5 miles round trip)
Level: Easy

Bathrooms nearby: Yes, in Springville there is a park in the center of town with restrooms
Water Temperature: Cold
Clothing Optional: No
Dog/Kid friendly: No
Best Season: July & August

The Middle Fork Tule River has some spectacular waterfalls and swimming holes. One of the best and easiest to access stretches of the Tule features this amazing 50-foot waterfall and swimming hole.

The swimming hole has jumps for all levels. Some of the young daredevils like to jump from the lip of the falls or even higher off the cliff. Cliff jumps probably go up to 120 feet. To get to the pool below, hike another 25 yards down past the falls.

The pool below is at least 8- to 10-feet deep. The water is a splendid aquamarine and pours off of the falls into a narrow chute that quickly and miraculously slows the water as it enters a 40 to 50 feet wide swimming hole. Entering the water is not as difficult as it might seem. The rocks look slippery and difficult to exit from the water. However, this is not the case.

Much of the rock is actually degraded granite providing for easy footing. The downstream portion of the hole is less shallow and provides for easy entrance to the deeper portions of the hole that start just below the chute of the falls.

There are ample ledges to catch some rays and some limited Manzanitas that provide shade along the river. Privacy is unlikely since this is a popular place.

This area and canyon can get quite hot. When we visited the temperature was about 112 degrees F. Bring extra water and plan accordingly since you are at reasonably high altitude.

Restaurant and Bathrooms:

The closest bathrooms are at the park located in the center of Springville, California.

Information and Contact:

There is a fee to enter this area. For a map of Sequoia National Forest, contact the office below or visit the website at www.fs.fed.us/r5/maps/. For further information please contact Giant Sequoia National Monument/Sequoia National Forest, Tule River Ranger District, 32588 Hwy. 190, Springville, CA 93265, 559-539-2607, website: www.r5.fs.fed.us/sequoia.

For additional photos and a video, please visit our website at:

http://swimmingholesofcalifornia.blogspot.com

Highlights

Plan ahead and stay overnight at the Hampton Inn in Tulare. California Hot Springs is just up the road if you are interested in spending a day at a hot springs also. There are also a number of other swimming holes nearby and easy to access.

MIDDLE FORK TULE RIVER FALLS

MIDDLE FORK TULE RIVER FALLS

Driving Directions:

From Porterville, drive east on Hwy. 190 for 18 miles to Springville. From Springville, continue on Hwy. 190 for 7.5 miles until you reach the powerhouse bridge and the exit to Camp Wishon and Wishon Dr. (Rd. 208). Cross the bridge and continue straight on Hwy. 190 up the mountain on the winding road for another 1.7 miles. The turnoff will be on the right. Prior to the turn off there is a view of the falls that is easy to miss. This will help given you an idea of the location. There is a forest service sign at the turnoff parking area. The trail is located to the right of the forest service sign at the bottom right side of the turnoff. The trail you will be hiking on is the Stevenson Trail. It is a somewhat well maintained and good trail. Follow it down until you come to a fork. You may be tempted to follow the fork and switchbacks to the left and down. If you do, you will reach Lilly's Lagoon instead. You will know you are on the wrong trail almost immediately since you will get a view of Lilly's Lagoon (a.k.a. Stevenson Gully). In order to reach the falls, continue straight on the trail across the face of the mountain slope. The lip of the falls is not fare and will be on your left. Hike down another 25 yards to reach the swimming hole and paradise!

THE CLIFFS

Sequoia National Park, off Hwy. 198 near the Southern Sierra Research Center
Access: Hike 0.25 miles one way (0.5 miles round trip)
Elevation: Starts at 2,900 feet; total loss about 100 feet
Level: Easy

Bathrooms nearby: Yes at the information center just up the road
Water Temperature: Moderate/Cold
Clothing Optional: No
Dog/Kid friendly: Yes
Best Season: May-September
Note: Although the hike is fairly easy, the trail down to the river is a little steep

The Cliffs is certainly a contender for one of the best swimming holes in the state of California. This swimming hole has largely been a best kept secret of locals. A small falls empties into a magnificent gorge channel that flows about half a mile and discharges into a large rock enclosed basin.

The basin at the end of the gorge channel has sandy beaches on both sides and easy access into the water. Further up the river into the channel, the rocks provide endless ledges for catching rays and jumping. Jumps range from low slabs to very high cliffs towering over 400 feet on the far side of the gorge. A favorite jumping spot is about half way up the gorge channel just near the falls. The cliff height is about 50 to 75 feet Some small jumps are just across the gorge from this jumping area. A favorite pass time of locals is to jump off the cliffs near the falls and float downstream until reaching the large basin. This can be done with or without an inner tube.

Further downstream from the large swimming basin are a number of rock slides that provide endless opportunities for fun. Still further down river are other swimming holes that provide more privacy.

Water quality is quite good although the swimming hole is just downstream from a waste water treatment plant. The brilliant emerald green color of the water and clarity make it hard to judge the depth which is at least 10 to 15 feet deep in most parts of the gorge and channel.

There are a number of small trees in close proximity to the swimming basin that provide ample shade for relaxing and reading a book. This canyon can get quite hot, so plan on packing a lunch with some extra water!

Given the ease of access to the swimming hole, privacy is unlikely.

Restaurant and Bathrooms:

The closest bathrooms are at the information center which is just up the road.

Information and Contact:

There is a fee to enter this area. For a map of Sequoia and Kings Canyon National Parks, contact the office or visit the website below. For further information please contact Sequoia and Kings Canyon National Park, Hwy. 198, Three Rivers, CA 93265, 559-565-3341, website: www.nps.gov/seki .

For additional photos and a video, please visit our website at:

http://swimmingholesofcalifornia.blogspot.com

Highlights

Plan ahead and stay overnight at the Hampton Inn in Visalia and Tulare. There are a number of swimming holes in close proximity to this one. Stop at the Gateway Restaurant in Three Rivers and have a nice lunch or dinner outside on the Kaweah River.

Driving Directions:

From Visalia, drive east on Hwy. 198 (Generals Hwy.) for about 37 miles to a turnoff just before the Southern Sierra Research Center (after you pay the fee and enter the park, but just before the Sequoia information center). The trail is fairly easy to spot and is just behind and to the right of the Southern Sierra Research Center. There is a large salty sinkhole to the right of the trail (the trail goes between the Southern Sierra Research Center and the sinkhole). Follow the trail for about 0.25 miles through a metal chain link fence. The trail then becomes steeper with a number of switchbacks. Follow the trail down until you reach the bottom. Continue to the left and upstream to reach the swimming areas.

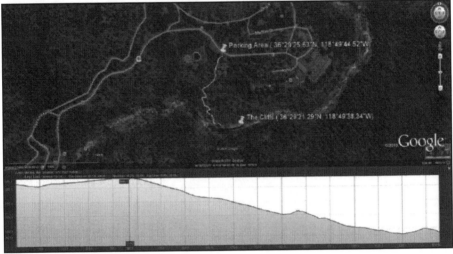

BIG SUR, SALINAS &
SANTA BARBARA

ARROYO SECO

Eastern Ventanna Wilderness near Salinas, California (Los Padres National Forest)
Access: Hike 3.5 miles one way (7.0 miles round trip) This is from the gate Add another 1.5 miles (3.0 miles both ways) if you hike from the day use area
Elevation: Starts at 2000 feet; total gain of 400 feet
Level: Moderate to strenuous with the added heat and lack of protection

Bathrooms nearby: Yes
Water Temperature: Cold
Clothing Optional: No
Dog/Kid friendly: Yes
Best Season: July, August, & September

Arroyo Seco is part of the Los Padres National Forest. It's under federal and not state management. For this reason this park remains open most of the year. However, a number of restrictions have been put in place to try to limit the number of hikers and swimmers that visit "The Gorge." The upper parking area will accommodate around 26 parked cars. The remainder are, therefore, required to park below in the day use area and hike up the road to the locked gate. This adds about 1.5 additional miles onto the hike (one way) or 3.0 miles total. The day use area has a few small swimming holes that are fun to splash around and play with the younger kids. This is a popular picnic area for the locals and can get quite crowded during the summer months. For this reason if you plan on visiting this park, you might want to get there early and get a reservation if you plan on camping.

Campers have designated parking places further up and closer to the gate. The gate was closed and locked a number of years ago requiring people to hike up to the "The Gorge" swimming hole. The road is quite narrow and dangerous and many fatalities have occurred by getting to close to the edge of the road. Although the road is quite wide many hikers seek to venture too close to the edge to their detriment.

The road traverses a 1000- to 2000-foot cliff and drop to the river. There is little shade along the road and hike to the "The Gorge." This makes the hike quite unpleasant and hot during the summer months. Plan ahead and bring extra water. Further, if you have parked in the day use area and weren't able to get one of the parking places, you will need to exit the area by 6 p.m. or your car will be locked in the parking lot. Although the road is fairly flat, the sun exposure is quite high making the hike from moderate to strenuous depending upon the time of year and day you do the hike. If you are adventurous you can hike or swim further up the canyon for another 1 to 2 miles to reach the Horse Bridge. From the Horse Bridge you can swim a couple more miles to where the "The Gorge" walls tighten. This is a dramatic and breathtaking area for swimming. There is also a 20-foot waterfall located in the same vicinity. There are ample ledges, jumps, and beach space located at the "The Gorge" area. Given the hike distance there will be some people, but probably not as many as in the past. At the far end of the "The Gorge" is a series of walls and ledges that provide for 30- to 40-foot jumps. Note that the trail down to the river is often marked by two "trash cans" and is fairly steep. You can see the beach and swimming area from the cliff above as you approach the swimming area. Bring a minimum of two bottles of water for the hike.

Restaurant and Bathrooms:

The closest bathrooms are in the day use parking area.

Information and Contact:

There is a charge to enter this park.

For additional photos and a video, please visit our website at:

http://swimmingholesofcalifornia.blogspot.com

Highlights

Bring along you sturdy floatation device and float down the river from the "The Gorge" to the day use area. This may require some limited "take outs" and boulder hopping, but can be quite fun.

ARROYO SECO

ARROYO SECO

Driving Directions:

Multiple swimming holes and jumping places on a 45-minute hike along a fire road that parallels the Arroyo Seco River. There is a developed National Forest camping area at Arroy Seco Campground. To get there, continue on Rt. 101 south past Salinas and exit at Greenfield and take Oak Ave. west for 1.5 miles, turn south (left) on 14th St. then quickly west (right) on Elm Ave. Go about 4.1 miles on Elm Ave. then turn left to stay on Rt. 16/Elm Ave. and continue about 7 more miles. Then a slight left (west) onto Arroyo Seco Rd. and go another 5 miles and park at the parking area above the Arroyo Seco Campground. Take the trail steeply uphill past the gate and continue on the fire road for about 3.5 miles to two trash cans that mark the trail down to the swimming area. Other swimming holes are along this stretch of the river and further up past the Horse Bridge.

Los Padres National Forest off Hwy. 1 near Gorda
on the Big Sur Coast
Access: Hike 0.8 miles round trip
Elevation: Starts at 270 feet; total gain 50 feet
Level: Easy

Bathrooms nearby: Yes, up the road
Water Temperature: Cold year round
Clothing Optional: Yes
Dog/Kid friendly: Yes, a flat walk uphill to the falls
Best Season: Year-round

The three best falls in Big Sur include McWay Falls, Limekiln Falls, and Salmon Falls. Salmon Falls is the only one having a swimming hole. If you have driven Hwy. 1 before, you probably drove right by the falls without even knowing it. However, the falls are visible from the road. The falls are very easy to reach and you will probably see other cars parked here on a weekday or weekend. The falls were named Salmon Creek Falls because of the beautiful Salmon color of the rocks behind the falls. There are a number of rocks for sitting and sunbathing. The water can be fairly cold even in the summer, so you may get the swimming hole all to yourself!

You may be tempted to take a few trails that aren't marked that appear closest to the creek (north side of the river and bridge. Most people will be parking and walking down toward the trailhead). One trail has a steep section and requires you to maneuver around a tree root near a dangerous trench and then cross a log bridge under a tree canopy. The other heads up the canyon wall to the left. The log bridge route will get you to the river and the falls. The other will take you to never-never land (don't go this way). It's much easier to just return safely back to the road and head further down (south) to the marked trailhead.

There is a lot of poison oak in the area heading up to the falls, so be careful!

Follow the trail for about 5 minutes until it comes to a clear area like a campsite and follow one of the small trails down to the creek. Alternatively, the trail can also travel up to a small cave area with campsite. There is an access way down that requires you to enter the cave and slide down a rock and then exit the cave. Be careful. It's great fun! This will take you to nearly the rock buttress at the base of the falls (described below).

To get to the base of the large falls will require you to either get wet by navigating through the river or to climb over a very large rock buttress. Climbing over the rock involves a few awkward maneuvers, but can be done, even by children. Salmon Creek Falls is about 120 feet high and is not easy to photograph (because it's so high and the canyon is so narrow to access the basin). The best spot to photograph the falls is probably on the top of the rock buttress. The water from the falls is split into two or more downward flowing streams by a large rock balanced at the top of the falls. This is a falls that evokes the response "Wow."

Restaurant and Bathrooms:

Bathrooms are located at the nearby town and restaurants.

Information and Contact:

There is no fee. For a map of Los Padres National Forest, please contact the office listed below or visit the website www.fs.fed.us/r5/maps/. For more information, contact Los Padres National Forest, Monterey Ranger District, 406 S. Mildred Ave., King City, CA 93930, 831/385-5434, website: www.fs.fed.us/r5/lospadres.

SALMON FALLS

Driving Directions:

Awesome waterfall near the south end of Big Sur area (Los Padres National Forest) with a great swimming hole in the pool at the bottom. Bathing suits may be optional. To get here, go way south on Rt. 1, 7.5 miles south of Gorda. There is a tight turn in the road with a large parking spot on the east side of the road. You can see the waterfall from the road. Park and look near the south side of the bridge for the Salmon Creek trailhead (you may have to hunt a bit for this, but it's marked). Follow the trail for about 5 minutes until it comes to a clear area like a campsite and follow one of the small trails down to the creek. You will tell you are on the right trail because it does not require "bush-whacking" to get to the falls. Alternately, simply follow the sound of the water, and you will arrive at the base of the falls.

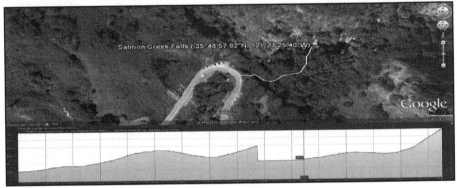

THE GORGE

Big Sur, just off of Hwy. 1
Access: Hike 0.25 miles one way (0.5 miles round trip)
Elevation: Starts at 1800 feet; total loss of 50 feet
Level: Easy

Bathrooms nearby: Yes
Water Temperature: Moderate
Clothing Optional: No
Dog/Kid friendly: Yes
Best Season: Good to visit all year round

Here is an easy place to reach that has just about everything you would expect from a great swimming hole. There is a nice beach and plenty of rocks to recline on. At the base of "The Gorge" is a nice size rock that you can try your luck to scale. The top of the rock is great to sit on, enjoy the view and relax.

Relative to other swimming holes, the water temperature is fairly moderate. More recently, the swimming hole has lost some depth due to increased amounts of sand being deposited at the base of the pool.

"The Gorge" comprises a funnel shaped pool that is about 60 feet wide and about the same in length. The swimming hole is positioned at the bottom of a gorge and is surrounded by 70-foot walls or higher on almost all sides. There is a small beach on the right side of "The Gorge" if you are facing up river. Water enters "The Gorge" through a small constriction at the base of the canyon.

You can try your luck and swim upstream to the large rocks that comprise the constriction. They provide a great vertical and horizontal element if you can make it.

Overall, this is a great place to visit if you are in Big Sur, Monterey, or Carmel. The restaurant and the lodge are also nice to visit and have ice cream and other treats available for small children.

Restaurant and Bathrooms:

The closest bathrooms and restaurants are at the Lodge as you drive in.

Information and Contact:

There is a fee to enter Pfeiffer-Big Sur State Park.

For additional photos, please visit our website at:

http://swimmingholesofcalifornia.blogspot.com

Highlights

You can take the kids to the swimming area just under the bridge that crosses the river. This is a popular place for families with small children. Pack a lunch and sit on the rocks with your significant other and enjoy the view.

THE GORGE

Driving Directions:

To get here, enter the Pfeiffer-Big Sur State Park. There is a charge to get into the park. Proceed to the lodge, which will be on your right. The lodge has a restaurant and bathrooms. There is also a general store there. At the fork near the lodge, bear left (it actually is the middle road) and follow this road along until you reach parking area #3 or #4. You will know you are on the correct road because the river will be on your right side. The correct parking for "The Gorge" is at the end of the road. At parking area #3 there is a paved path with a sign indicating that "The Gorge" is 0.6 miles. Follow the paved path up the hill until you reach the river. There is a plank bridge to cross the river. After crossing the river, follow the road to the left through the camping area until you reach a clearly marked trail. Follow the trail up the river for about 0.2 miles. Note that the best approach is to stay to the right. The path will take you almost all the way to "The Gorge." You will reach a point you can't go any further and will have to drop straight down into the river (there is a log you must climb over). Most people remove their shoes here. At this point you will need to cross the river to the other side. It's shallow enough to wade across. The water is not too deep here. The trail continues on the left side, until you reach the rock impound at the base of "The Gorge." If you follow these directions, you will only need to cross the river once and will not need to boulder hop. If you cross too early on the left side you may have to boulder hop or cross back in a deep section of the river. Note: There is no jumping at "The Gorge." Also, recently there have been significant deposits of sand on the bottom of "The Gorge" area making it shallower than in 2009. The only deep section now is on the side of "The Gorge" near the rock impound. It's about 8 to 10 feet deep. However, the good news is there is more beach area for chairs.

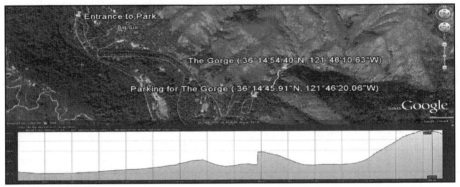

THE GORGE

About The Author

Timothy H. Joyce is an avid hiker and award-winning photographer. Tim's hiking group "HSG" or "Hiking and Swimming Hole Group," visits swimming holes and waterfalls throughout the year. He has been leading non-profit and charitable hikes for more than 10 years. If you would like to join one of the HSG hikes or subscribe to the free HSG weekly newsletter, please contact thjoyce@peoplepc.com.

Also, feel free to write us to share your swimming hole stories, and new or recent discoveries.

Index

Made in the USA
San Bernardino, CA
11 March 2016